Love and Terror in the Third Reich

Love and Terror in the
THIRD REICH

A Tale of Broken Integrity

Peter Matheson *and*
Heinke Sommer-Matheson

Foreword by William F. Storrar

CASCADE *Books* • Eugene, Oregon

LOVE AND TERROR IN THE THIRD REICH
A Tale of Broken Integrity

Copyright © 2019 Peter Matheson and Heinke Sommer-Matheson. All rights reserved. Except for brief quotations in critical publications or reviews, no part of this book may be reproduced in any manner without prior written permission from the publisher. Write: Permissions, Wipf and Stock Publishers, 199 W. 8th Ave., Suite 3, Eugene, OR 97401.

Cascade Books
An Imprint of Wipf and Stock Publishers
199 W. 8th Ave., Suite 3
Eugene, OR 97401

www.wipfandstock.com

PAPERBACK ISBN: 978-1-5326-6118-1
HARDCOVER ISBN: 978-1-5326-6119-8
EBOOK ISBN: 978-1-5326-6120-4

Cataloguing-in-Publication data:

Names: Matheson, Peter, author. | Sommer-Matheson, Heinke, author. | Storrar, William F., foreword.

Title: Love and terror in the Third Reich : a tale of broken integrity / Peter Matheson and Heinke Sommer-Matheson ; foreword by William F. Storrar.

Description: Eugene, OR: Cascade Books, 2019. | Includes bibliographical references.

Identifiers: ISBN: 978-1-5326-6118-1 (paperback). | ISBN: 978-1-5326-6119-8 (hardcover). | ISBN: 978-1-5326-6120-4 (epub).

Subjects: LCSH: Soldiers—Germany—Correspondence.| World War, 1939–1945—Personal narratives, German. | Germany—History—1933–1945.

Classification: D811.A2 M 2019 (print). | D811.A2 (epub).

Manufactured in the U.S.A.   MARCH 19, 2019

To our parents, our children, and our grandchildren

Contents

Foreword by William F. Storrar | ix
Acknowledgments | xiii
Abbreviations | xv
Chronology | xvii
Prologue | xix
Maps | xxvii

1. Childhood, Youth, Marriage | 1
2. The False Sense of Peace | 24
3. Why Hitler? Why National Socialism? | 41

The Photos | 60

4. Russia | 69
5. The Last Days | 103
6. The Special Significance of Letters | 114
Conclusion | 129

Afterword: A Personal Pilgrimage | 135
Appendix: Family Tree | 141
Bibliography | 143

Foreword

WE LIVE IN A disturbing moment in European history. We see the alarming acceptance in the media and public life of racist and anti-immigrant rhetoric by elected politicians and government leaders. Bullies that they are, they rage against the most vulnerable in European society, indifferent to the rise in hate crimes with their every jugular or jocular utterance against refugees, migrants, veiled Muslim women, and Jewish citizens. This was something unthinkable in the decades after the Second World War and Holocaust for all but a squalid handful of backstreet thugs and their gang leaders on the violent fringes of electoral politics. Yet we are now witnessing the enactment of these very same ethnic nationalist prejudices by democratically elected governments that brazenly employ such populist hate speech across the Continent. Those of us who naively believed that postwar Europe was the new heartland and hope of liberal democracy, the rule of law, human rights, and transnational cooperation in the world are bewildered by the rapidity and ferocity of this change in the European political climate within a mere decade of the global financial crash in 2008. How could this happen, we ask?

We are like the accident victims staggering in shock out of a wrecked family car. It seemed so safe as we daydreamed our way along a familiar route to a known destination, only to find ourselves skidding out of control in a sudden downpour of racist bile on the public highway. There are many reasons for this current collapse of public decency in Europe, but the loss of recent historical memory is threaded through them all. In the early 1990s I was an academic observer at the congress of the European People's Party in Brussels, sitting with the Dutch Christian Democrat delegation in this meeting of the center-right political parties in the European Parliament. I vividly remember the then German Chancellor Helmut Kohl's speech to the congress. Without mentioning her by name, he spoke of those like the

Foreword

British prime minister Margaret Thatcher, who saw closer European cooperation as a threat to national sovereignty. "Idioten!" he cried, and then turned warmly to his friend Leo Tindemans, a former prime minister of Belgium, and said in effect, "Leo, we shall never forget meeting after the war as young Christian Democrats amid the ruins of a divided Europe, destroyed by nationalism. We determined then, Never again!" Sadly, with the passing of that young wartime generation, Europe has forgotten, and it is happening again. The *idioten* are not only on the streets once more. They are back in power. That is why this extraordinary book is so timely. It asks the same question: How could such things happen?

"What was it that led ordinary, caring people to see Hitler as their saviour, to embrace apocalyptic dreams of revenge and conquest which swept aside all sobriety, rationality, and morality?" With this disturbing question Peter and Heinke take us immediately to the heart of the heartrending story they have translated and told here with breathtaking candour. They show us how a devout young Christian couple's loving and tender correspondence in wartime Europe is marbled through with devotion to the Nazi cause. The couple in question, Lilo and Ernst, are none other than Heinke's parents and Peter's in-laws. The authors have thus achieved the delicate and brave feat of combining critical scholarship (in documenting this unholy allegiance) with compassionate empathy for their loved ones: so close to them in human flesh, and yet so far from them in political values. Lilo and Ernst's translators and interpreters have done nothing less than tell the truth in love. In these pages they show us how to do so with integrity. For this is not the lurid exposé of a skeleton in the family closet, but the painstaking restoration of a self-portrait in words by two fine people of faith who yet wore the swastika with pride. "What are we to make of it all?", the authors ask of their loved ones' letters, and prompt us to ask in turn.

The Scottish writer George Gunn has commented on the return of racism in contemporary British public life by quoting the ancient Roman historian Suetonius. In his biography of Caligula there comes a turning point when Suetonius says, "So much for Gaius the Emperor; the rest of this history must needs deal with Gaius the Monster." *Love and Terror in the Third Reich* is not about two monstrous Nazis, but it does help us to understand how Germany turned from a constitutional republic into the totalitarian fiefdom of Hitler the Monster, precisely through the enchantment of evil under the guise of national emancipation. Yet our Christian couple cannot escape moral responsibility for the Nazi loyalties in their

Foreword

correspondence. Their love letters are a cameo of a complex history that must needs deal with the Monster of National Socialism. In his account of how the birthplace of Goethe and Beethoven became the builder of Belsen and Buchenwald, the German sociologist Wolf Lepenies concludes that Hitler was able to seduce Germany into the abyss because ordinary people did not speak out in protest *the very first time* their neighbor or colleague was vilified or taken away: ordinary people like Lilo and Ernst. It was then the Monster knew the fabric of decency was rent asunder and the terror could begin. The same holds true in Europe today. Heinke and Peter enable us to understand this deal with the devil, then and now. Lest we forget.

William F. Storrar
Director
Center for Theological Inquiry
Princeton, New Jersey

Acknowledgments

THIS BOOK HAD A long genesis, and many debts have been incurred on the way: to computer technicians and advisers, and to friends and encouragers. We cannot name them all, but would single out Heather Cameron, Kevin Clements, Lindsay Matheson, Andrew Schuller, Brett Knowles, John Miller, Will Storrar, and the editors and staff of Cascade Books, who offer a rare combination of efficiency and human warmth. This book would not be here without them. Our heartfelt thanks go to all of them.

Heinke Sommer-Matheson
Peter Matheson

Abbreviations

NCO	Noncomissioned officer
RAF	Royal Air Force
SS	*Schutzstaffel* (lit. Protection Squadron)

Chronology

12 September 1912	Ernst Sommer born in Wienboeken, Schleswig-Holstein
4 August 1913	Lilo Struck born in Spantekow, Mecklenburg, Hither Pomerania
1914–1919	*First World War*
1916	Death of Ernst's father, August, prisoner of war in Rumania
1920	*National Socialist Party founded*
1929–1938	*Great Depression*
30 January 1933	*Hitler Chancellor of Germany*
September 1935	*Nuremberg Laws*
31 December 1935	Ernst Sommer and Lilo Struck engaged
March 1936	*German troops march into the Rhineland*
September 1937	Ernst passes final exams as teacher
11 March 1938	Ernst and Lilo married; live in Wrohm, Schleswig-Holstein
12 March 1938	*Austria incorporated into Third Reich*
30 September 1938	*Munich Agreement; Annexation of Sudetenland*
9 November 1938	*"Crystal Night"; Synagogues in flames*
12 February 1939	Birth of daughter, Heinke
March 1939	*Invasion of Czechoslovakia*
July 1939	Ernst called up to Army

CHRONOLOGY

1 September 1939	*Invasion of Poland; Second World War begins*
10 March 1940	Birth of son, Hartmut
May–August 1940	Ernst in officer training school, Potsdam
10 May 1940	*Invasion of Low Countries and France*
23 August 1940	*Soviet–German Non-Aggression Pact*
December 1940	Ernst in Pornic, Bretagne, in occupied France
March–May 1941	Ernst in Graudenz/Grudziadz, Poland, then in Tilsit, East Prussia
22 June 1941	*Invasion of Russia*
June 1941—February 1942	Ernst engaged in battles around Staraja Russa, Russia
21 July 1941	Lilo flees from bombing of Wrohm to Pomerania
15 January 1942	Death of Ernst's brother, Hans
11 February 1942	Death of Ernst at Borki, near Staraja Russa, Russia
13 October 1943	Death of Lilo's brother, Hans-Dieter
March 1945	Lilo and her children flee from Hither Pomerania to Schleswig-Holstein
September 2001	Heinke Sommer-Matheson travels to Staraja Russa and Borki
22 August 2005	Lilo Sommer dies
30 August 2005	Heinke discovers her parents' letters

Prologue

It is shocking that day after day naked acts of violence, breaches of the law, barbaric opinions appear quite undisguised as official decree.
—VICTOR KLEMPERER, MARCH 1933

THE GROUNDSWELL OF SUPPORT that made National Socialism possible surged out of ordinary homes. What was it that led ordinary, caring people to see Hitler as their savior, to embrace apocalyptic dreams of revenge and conquest which swept aside all sobriety, rationality, and morality? A treasure trove of more than a thousand letters and postcards, the conversation between one ordinary young couple, Liselotte (Lilo) and Ernst Sommer, together with their books, songs, and photos, throws a unique light on this question.

These letters, written in the obscure Sütterlin script, have been transcribed by their daughter, Heinke Sommer-Matheson, now living in New Zealand. In their intimacy, their frankness, and their innocence, the letters between the young lovers offer a unique window into the world of young people in Hitler's Germany. What was it like to grow up in the wake of the First World War? What drew Ernst and Lilo into the Hitler Youth and its female counterpart, and why did they throw themselves with such enthusiasm into Nazi programs such as the *Landjahr* (the Year on the Land)? We read of them working eighteen-hour days. We see them burning the candle at both ends. What songs did they sing, what films did they watch, and what dreams did they have for their personal future? We will get to know Ernst and Lilo as caring, loving, and thoughtful people. So how on earth did they miss the dark sides to the National Socialist program, how did they shrug aside its violence, its expansionist plans, its preparations for war, its ethnocentrism, and its anti-Semitism? Why did the rhetoric of Goebbels and the Führer enthrall them as they and their families gathered around the radio?

As we read their letters, we will find ourselves walking into an alien world. The life that Ernst and Lilo lived in their little villages at opposite ends of North Germany was unimaginably different from the life of today. Life revolved around the seasons. It was simple, elemental, and could be raw and demanding. Women faced a weekly and yearly round of mending and washing, cooking and gardening, preserving fruit, and looking after the kids. Village life was basically a subsistence economy. There was of course no whiteware in the kitchen; there were no supermarkets and no flush toilets; one fired up the stove to keep warm. One walked, bicycled everywhere, or took the train. On occasion Ernst cycled right through the night to reach home. And into this traditional way of life stormed National Socialism, which was experienced by them both as a liberating revolution, but which also brought with it all manner of new obligations.

It takes us a huge leap of imagination to begin to enter this world. The Party controlled all the media outlets: radio, newspapers, magazines, films, and all the professional organizations. Ernst and Lilo had no contacts at all with differing views—with traditional conservatives, or with liberal, trade unionist, or socialist groups. On the contrary their early letters to one another brim with idealism and hope for the future. Lilo once saw Hitler face-to-face. She and her group of girls, standing by the roadside, were dressed in the uniform of the *Landjahr*. Hitler's eyes caught the pennant they carried. They had spent the night sewing it, and now it had been "honored by his glance." It was a "brief but unforgettable moment."[1] Hitler had this intuitive, magnetic ability to connect with the young.

Ernst bought his beloved violin[2] from a gypsy, and his expensive dress sword when he was promoted to lieutenant. He loved music and thrilled to the challenge of fighting for his country. Culture and National Socialist values were a seamless robe for him.

Lilo was in her element when dancing, swimming, camping, and singing. She was a keen gymnast. For her the "new Germany" of Hitler opened up a pathway to health and happiness for all; she threw herself into working with the Party's organizations for young women. She believed it would

---

1. Lilo to Ernst, May 30, 1935.
2. Ernst to Lilo, June 2, 1937.

Prologue

equip girls to enjoy life, to develop their skills, to live for the good of the whole community.

Ernst, who was a young teacher in two village schools, joined the SA, and led the Hitler Youth movement in his area in its marches, camps, and overseas trips. With the benefit of tertiary education, he was more of a systematic thinker than Lilo. As he put it himself, he was a *Grübler* (worrier), pondering a whole host of issues, reading widely in history and psychology, and trying to make sense of his life and that of his nation. He had a deep religious faith that complemented his enthusiasm for National Socialism. He was committed to the building up of community life, to promoting the life of the spirit, and to the geopolitical strategies of the Party. He was also passionate about bringing out the best in his pupils, infecting them with his love for the region, for forest and field and bird life, and for music and traditional folk songs, as well as the three *r*'s. He was not at all what we expect when we think of a Nazi. Nor was Lilo.

More than seventy years later their daughter came across the asymmetric witness of their letters. It proved to be an epochal voyage of discovery for her:

While engaged in the sad business of clearing away and sorting out my mother's things after her death in 2005 I came across a big wooden box in the wardrobe. I had seen it before but didn't know what was in it. Now as I slid back the lid, I was flabbergasted to see that it contained countless letters, mountains of them.

Hartmut, my brother, had known more about the correspondence than me. But for him the letters were profoundly private artifacts, belonging only to our parents, Ernst and Lilo, letters of love and grief, and reassurance. No way should they be seen by others. For me, too, it has always been an ethical issue that I might be intruding on my parents' inner life.

Anyway I took them back with me to New Zealand when I returned there, crammed into that big, heavy box. For a long time I did nothing with them, because I was not at all sure what, if anything, I should be doing. The Sütterlin script in which they were written was alienating, quite foreign to me. I could not make head or tail of it. My mother had typed out one of the letters, though, which contained my father's reflections in 1939 when he heard that war had broken out. "Es ist Krieg," he had written, "it's war, then." On leave from his army training course in Wrohm, the village in Schleswig-Holstein where he was the teacher, he had sat up late into the night and put

Prologue

his thoughts and feelings into words. Obviously it was a crucial letter for my mother so she had typed it out. I wondered why. For whom was it meant?

So this typed letter, grim and ominous as it was, offered me a way in. I began to be curious about the other letters. I had been profoundly moved by a visit to Russia, to see where my father had fallen. I had also been contacted by a Dutch oral historian who was interested in the reactions of the children of fallen German soldiers. Her work made me realize how little I knew of my father. I was ashamed, too, that I knew nothing of the Westerborg Sammellager, where the Dutch Jews had been herded together prior to being taken to the East to their death, and had never heard about the Dutch people who had worked with Jewish survivors from the Third Reich. I was now reading more and more books about the course of the War, about anti-Semitism, and about the generation of folk in middle age, like me, who had lost their fathers in the War. Ulla Hahn's novel "Unscharfe Bilder" ("Hazy Images"), about the silences and misunderstandings between my father's generation and my own made a deep impression on me. My parents' songbooks and storybooks from their own childhood were on our bookshelves. My mother's photo albums conjured up a family history going right back to solemn great-grandparents, family celebrations, my own childhood, and my young, radiantly happy mother; above all the father I had never had the chance to talk to: Ernst as a boy, a student, a teacher, and in the uniform of the Wehrmacht, in that terrible Russian winter. Snapshots of reality, of a world I knew nothing about. All this was simmering away inside me. I had dragged the heavy box all the way with me to New Zealand. It sat there, and became a sort of challenge to me. The letters needed to be read, if only to satisfy my curiosity.

Initially it was incredibly difficult, slow, slow work to decipher them. I had to sort the letters chronologically, and separate out Ernst's letters from Lilo's. Initially I could spend a whole hour on one sentence; lots of places and people's names I couldn't decipher at all. Until I began to get used to the script—my father's sloping handwriting was particularly difficult to read—I could spend hours poring over one or two paragraphs, and still there were countless gaps, names of places or people I could not decipher, questionable readings. I made some dreadful mistakes, guessing my way through difficult sections.

Yet from that very first typed letter all sorts of questions accompanied my attempts to transcribe them. What had motivated my father or mother to act as they did, to say this or that? Much of the content was emotionally disturbing. I remember saying to myself: "Don't do this! You'll just get deeper

Prologue

and deeper into intimate, private realms Lilo and Ernst would never have wanted you to explore."

But I was hooked. I needed to unravel the mystery around their daily struggles, their commitment to National Socialism, and their passionate relationship to one another. I was stubborn and didn't want to be defeated. I began to realize how dependent Lilo was on Ernst, how he could mold her, stimulate her intellectually, and support her emotionally. I knew of course of her fierce loyalty to the memory of her dead husband. Now I could begin to put flesh on that skeleton.

My work with the letters went in fits and starts. It extended over years. Other priorities interrupted it. There were major health issues I had to cope with, including breast cancer; I had to move house. But the letters did not go away. I began sorting out the quite extensive collection of photos from my childhood, and from the War, for my children's sake as well. I wrote up my "pilgrimage" to Russia. My cousin Ernst Otto and his wife were busy writing their family chronicle, and sent me more letters between his mother, Leni, and Ernst. All this was quietly encouraging.

So I realized that the work had to be done and could be done. The letters would offer me a detailed and emotionally honest entrance into the life and thinking of my father and of my mother. It was not good enough just to dabble. I had to transcribe the lot, all these hundreds of letters, postcards, these traces of another world. I had lost my father as a three-year-old; now my mother had died, and these letters were all I had left of them both.

To my surprise I discovered a different mother. A completely new picture of her began to emerge. I was surprised at her fierce determination to bring to an end the long, long engagement to Ernst, her decisiveness in overcoming the resistance of Ernst's family to the marriage. I was startled to find how strongly she came to hate the war. I also felt immense pity for her. Mein Gott, what had she gone through, suffered, mostly alone, without anyone to talk things through with, no one to lean on.

Stubbornness kept me at the transcribing, though I often felt it was too demanding on me, emotionally and intellectually, and very time consuming. I certainly didn't see myself as a historian, but I was gradually building up a picture, for example, of their life in the village of Wrohm as the schoolteacher and his wife; a picture of the house, the vegetable garden, the community life there; and a picture of myself as a small child. Who was I, who was this child? It was extraordinary in how much detail Ernst wanted to know about everything when he was away in France or Russia; about his daughter, Heinke (myself), and his little son, Hartmut; about the vocabulary and language skills I was accumulating; about my little adventures, and all the childhood illnesses. Here in the letters I could draw on and benefit from all this information about this lost world.

So much was new to me, including the remarkable depth of love between Lilo and Ernst. This was obvious from the frequency of their letters and parcels, the passionate language they used, and their deep practical concern for each other. New to me also were the fierce conflicts that sometimes broke out between them. I became sharply aware of the cruelty and waste of the War and how it wreaked havoc on this little family.

I am inclined to say that the letters brought me closer to Ernst than to Lilo. Apart from his photo on the piano my father had been unknown to me, a remote, iconic figure. But now I could see that as a husband he remained an ardent lover; he was so proud of Lilo, his thoughts constantly circling around her. He was contemptuous of other officers who were disloyal to their wives, though the long separation was very difficult for him. He was supportive of her, and insisted on being there at my birth, pretty unusual at the time. He constantly gave her advice about the children's development, their occasional tantrums, explaining that this was all natural. He seems to have thought day and night about me and Hartmut.

I felt cheated, quite angry, really, that as a teacher myself I never had the chance to experience his pedagogic skills. Obviously he was a natural, a brilliant teacher, with his love of music and nature, of poetry, and of the history and traditions, the lore and language of Schleswig-Holstein where he grew up.

I could never identify, however, with his fierce loyalty to the "New Germany," to the Führer, with his profound sense of duty, and with his unquestioning patriotism. All this left me cold, though I didn't feel anger about this soldier father of mine. I never saw him as "a Nazi." In a sense he had a wider framework of concern than Lilo, not only for his own career and family, but this overweening sense of duty and responsibility for Germany.

The letters prompted a quest for my own identity. What had this War done to me, robbing me of my father, of all that inner security? Again and again, too, I felt remorse that I hadn't done more for my mother, knowing as I did now all she had been through.

At times working on the letters was too much for me emotionally, especially the last letters before his death, around Christmas 1941 and early in the New Year, and Lilo's last letters to him, sent off to a husband already cold in the ground. For a month I shied away from them. My mother's loneliness

Prologue

got to me, her sleeplessness, and her despair. Worst of all were the death announcements in the newspapers, lauding his heroic death for the Fatherland, and the warm but terrible letters of consolation from his erstwhile fellow officers and comrades.

I have spent thousands of hours on these letters. It has been a labor of love. I am now not only infinitely better informed, but much prouder of my parents, aware of their integrity, their determination to do their best for us children, their fierce fight for what they believed to be right. Torn apart by war, deceived by their betters, they were ordinary people in extraordinary times.

It is not easy for me to disentangle what I have learned from the letters about life during the Third Reich from what I have learned from countless, books, films, other people's accounts, my own Jewish friends, and my visit to Israel. All these have shaped my thinking. I suppose, though, that the letters and postcards, the photos, and the descriptions of the parcels they sent to one another brought things down to earth for me, rooted them in individual and family reality. I could now identify through the letters with Lilo's anxiety and fear, especially for her two little children, as bombs rained down on her little village. Previously I had only a sketchy idea of what the bombing was like. As woman to woman I could now feel for my mother. I could identify with my father's accounts of the forced marches through the night to reach the Russian border, the comradeship with his men as they built the block house in the forest, and the incredible incident when he and his brother, Hans, met in East Prussia, grabbed bikes, frolicked naked together in the little river, sang and hallooed together. It made him real. As Ernst Otto, my cousin, commented: "Only the Sommers could do that." All this was so new to me.

I began, too, to realize how limited their knowledge and insight into events were, dependent as everyone was on the official propaganda. I noted, though, how soon Lilo's early elation at the victories in Poland and France gave way to stress, tension, fear, and drastic loss of weight as she heard that Ernst was off to Russia. She was a worrier, but in many ways this made her judgement on the course of the War more realistic than the sanguine pronouncements of my father. Her letters, with their heartfelt concern for his health, his dental care, his protection from a ferocious winter, and above all his survival brought the reality of life at the Front home to me. Many of my questions, however, still remain unanswered.

Uncertain about what was actually happening in Russia, my mother learned from other soldiers' wives about the terrible scenes in the field

PROLOGUE

hospitals, and the growing list of fatalities. Here were other women who understood her anxiety about Ernst. It was not enough for her to accept what was said in the papers or the radio. So, personal exchanges and experiences crisscrossed the official propaganda. She could not understand, for example, the Army's failure to clothe the men at the Front. Surely the Army should have known about the Russian winter. Everyone knew about Napoleon! Like so many women called upon by Goebbels to knit socks and to provide warm clothing, she began to question the competence of the army planning.

It's clear from the letters that Ernst took her anxieties seriously, but his basic attitude was that of a false protectiveness. In the end his glossing over the difficulties and dangers infuriated Lilo, although in part of her mind the maturity, thoughtfulness and wisdom of Ernst remained unquestioned. He was more than a little concerned, too, at Lilo's flouting of military censorship and secrecy and her desire to know exactly where he was.

In conclusion I continue to be overwhelmed by the quantity, the realistic detail, and the profound affection displayed in the letters. For different reasons, both partners needed to be reaffirmed about their love for one another. These letters kept this love alive for me as well.

Maps

MAP 1

Title: Map of Schleswig-Holstein, administrative divisions (identifying Wrohm, Heide, and Schalkholtz).
Author: TUBS: https://commons.wikimedia.org/wiki/User:TUBS
Created on August 22, 2012
https://commons.wikimedia.org/wiki/File:Schleswig-Holstein,_administrative_divisions_-_de_-_colored.svg
This file is licensed under the GNU Free Documentation License

Maps

MAP 2

Title: Locator map of counties in Mecklenburg-Vorpommern,
Germany after country reorganization 2011
(identifying Anklam, Spantikow, and Swinemunde)
Author: TUBS: https://commons.wikimedia.org/wiki/User:TUBS
Created on July 23, 2009
https://commons.wikimedia.org/wiki/File:Mecklenburg-Vorpommern
_districts_2011_colored_labeled.svg/.
This file is licensed under the GNU Free Documentation License

Maps

MAP 3

Title: Outline Map of Novgorod Oblast
Author: Виктор В
Created on September 4, 2010.
https://commons.wikimedia.org/wiki/File:Outline_Map_of
_Novgorod_Oblast.svg#mw-jump-to-license/.

This file is licensed under the Creative Commons
Attribution-Share Alike 2.0 Generic license.

1

Childhood, Youth, and Marriage

Although you are far apart from one another, physically, you can still be present through letters and writing, in this way talking and opening up your heart to another.

—MARTIN LUTHER, 1539[1]

When we think of the Third Reich what comes to mind first of all is its supermarket of horrors, its totalitarianism and nihilism, the Führer, Adolf Hitler, and his cronies. Yet this focus on the macro scene, on Nuremberg rallies, propaganda extravaganzas, on *Blitzkrieg* and the sadism of Auschwitz may miss the abyss of human and social tragedy that characterized the Hitler era. The subtlety and radicality of evil in the Third Reich is even more evident in the intimacy of individual and family stories, in its perversion of the love and idealism of the young. For the personal and the political walked hand in hand. Hitler, let's remember, was seen as the infallible authority on family and womanhood as well as everything else! Domesticity as well as geopolitics was meant to be refashioned by the New Reich (Empire).

Between the strutting Gauleiters and the luftmenschen, the spectral humans of the concentration camps, lay strata upon strata of apparent ordinariness: devoted mothers and homemakers, young folk drawn into a new world of companionship and idealism, and teachers reaching out to

---

1. *Tischreden (Table Talk)*, quoted by Ernst Sommer, January 30, 1941; we do not know what collection of quotations Ernst had at his disposal.

their pupils with recorder and folk song. The evil of the Third Reich certainly lay in its brutality and ruthlessness, its trampling moral and religious values underfoot, but it was at its most perverse in its harnessing of the well-meaning for demonic outcomes. *Corruptio optimi pessima* (nothing worse than the seduction of the good).

Family photo albums, diaries, children's books, and cheap editions of the centuries of German poetry and literature and song take us into the homes of ordinary people living through this time of upheaval. Ernst and Lilo lived parsimoniously, on the smell of an oily rag, but a piano was an absolute priority for them. Their culture was a rich and warm one, a very human one, though its syncretism is bewildering. Side by side on the family shelves sat the Bible, Schiller, *Mein Kampf*, and Rosenberg's racist *Der Mythus des 20. Jahrhunderts (Myth of the Twentieth Century)*, all now regarded as classics. Ernst Sommer talked of his pleasure in learning from *den Alten* (the old ones); he found there his spiritual sustenance, "whether it was from Jesus, Kant, Schiller or Rosenberg."[2] This is not untypical. Around the piano in countless village halls Lutheran hymns mingled with lilting folk music and the rousing marches from the Hitler Youth songbook. In winter children huddled around the stove, listening to Hans Christian Andersen's fairy tales, Mark Twain's yarns, and the adventures of Karl May, intertwined with heroic sagas from the Great War.[3] The well-thumbed poetry books of Ernst and Lilo testify to the rich treasury of German literature stretching back to the Middle Ages. Countless poems were learnt off by heart.

The letters of Ernst and Lilo open up this world to us. The young lovers wrote to one another almost every second day, and the frequency of their letters, of their parcels and photos, documents their deep concern for every aspect of their partner's life. We learn about their meals, their illnesses, and their family gatherings. During his military service Ernst would regularly bundle up Lilo's previous letters, stored up to then in the saddlebag of his horse, Titus, and send them back to Lilo, so that they could read them together after the war. They often thought ahead to the postwar period.[4] They were aware that the separation induced by the war, and their vastly different experiences of young motherhood and village life, on the one hand, and the privations and brutality of the Front, on the other, was changing them,

---

2. Ernst to Lilo, November 4, 1935.

3. Of course, a glance at Arthur Mee's *Children's Encyclopaedia* reminds us of a not altogether dissimilar cultural mishmash in the British scene.

4. Lilo to Ernst, June 5, 1941.

Childhood, Youth, and Marriage

driving a wedge between them, and threatening to pull them apart. The assiduous letter writing was a deliberate strategy to prevent this happening.[5]

Tragically, this retrospective rereading was never to take place. Yet, miraculously, the letters themselves did survive, were somehow preserved by Lilo through the utter chaos at the war's end, which included a pell-mell flight with two small children from Pomerania to the west. For decades the letters were kept in a large brown box in a wardrobe. Lilo herself could not bear to read them until 1980. She had tried to do so many times, but it had simply been too painful. "It is so emotionally demanding, my eyes swim with tears, but I am determined to face up to this most precious time in my life. You can't put into words what an impact, what an effect, what memories and emotions these written words generate. They document an unspeakably happy marriage and the immense love and care which surrounded me."[6]

Their correspondence began in 1935, with their falling in love, followed by a long engagement, and their eventual marriage. They lived, for much of their lives, at opposite ends of Germany—hence the abundance of letters, which at first offer a vivid window onto their early married life in Wrohm, a little village in Schleswig-Holstein away up in the north of Germany; and into their very different families: his in Hamburg and various villages in Schleswig-Holstein, and hers in the east, in far-off Pomerania. They are love letters, first in peace, then in war. For them their love was special, uniquely wonderful. The world had never been anything like it! All lovers may feel this. There is, however, something quite striking about this young couple.

Ernst and Lilo Sommer were in their late twenties when war broke out. What was it like for young people like them, their lives just beginning, to be caught up in the vast political and military dramas of the Second World War? Married at long last in March 1938 after an extended engagement, they were almost immediately wrenched apart by mobilization, by the campaign in France, and then by Operation Barbarossa, the Russian campaign.

Both had been enthusiastically involved in the National Socialist youth movements and came from Christian backgrounds. The letters offer a vivid account of Ernst's élan as a primary teacher and surprising insights

---

5. Lilo reflects about the way "many married people become estranged from one another. War is the worst thing on earth." Lilo to Ernst, September 11, 1940.

6. Lilo to Heinke Sommer-Matheson, February 3, 1980.

into his officer training. We overhear their excitement about the successes of Hitler's foreign policy, their pride that Germany was standing tall in the world again. Their delight in one another, in the birth and infancy of their two children, flows seamlessly into their enthusiasm for the new Germany, and their admiration of the genius of the Führer. Both were deeply affected, as countless letters testify, by the adroit symbolism of the National Socialist movement: its carefully choreographed mass gatherings, its gymnastic displays, and the drama of the raising and lowering of the flag—at dawn, at dusk, in the snow, and in wind and rain. While both of them were alert to the excesses such displays of emotion could generate, they were swept along, like millions of others, by a tide of hopefulness. A new age was at hand, and they were participants in its emergence.

From our perspective today the clouds of war were already gathering by the late 1930s, but there is scarcely a hint of this in their early letters. Hitler, they were sure, would steer the ship of state to a safe harbor. But then war *did* break out. Ernst left for garrison duty in coastal France, and then was posted to Russia. Bombs rained down on Lilo's village of Wrohm, and as casualties mounted in Russia, her anxiety escalates about what she now came to see as a quite ghastly war. To the very end, though, until his death in Borki, an obscure Russian village, on the eve of his daughter's third birthday, Ernst Sommer remained the caring spouse and father, the resolute comforter, and the confident believer in the *Endsieg* (final victory). Lilo, however, was left alone in 1942 with her two little children, amid the ruins of her hopes and dreams. She had eventually to cope with the death of husband, father, brother, and of virtually all her male relatives. The married life that had begun with such high hopes, personally and nationally, ended in comprehensive tragedy. It was not to end, either, in 1945, in *Jahr Null* (year nothing). The trail of letters peters out. The pain, the struggle, and the awesome questions—political and personal—had only just begun for mother and children.

This, then, is the record of a love story that swings from remote villages up in the north of Germany to officer training camps on the Baltic, then over to occupied France, and ends in the grim fighting on the Russian Front. We will be reading their intimate letters, raw and open in their ecstasy and pain, at times written in extremis, never intended for any eyes but theirs themselves. What gloves should we don as we handle them? What ethical rights have we to look over their shoulders?

Childhood, Youth, and Marriage

Lilo Struck and Ernst Sommer had fallen passionately in love with each other, yet shared a passionate commitment to the new Germany. They cherished their Christian faith but believed fervently in the mission of National Socialism and in its Führer, Adolf Hitler. They were young, committed people with soaring hopes. Their hundreds of letters to one another witness to the continual intersection of these public and familial worlds, to the vast political and military upheavals they lived though, and to their wonder and delight as lovers and parents.[7] Their social and personal roles as parents and lovers were inextricably bound up with a catastrophic misreading of cultural and political reality.

Their life together, his death, and her lifelong widowhood pose cruelly difficult questions: How can the ordinary people of a country at war keep their feet, retain integrity, and remain true to one another amid the whirlwind of geopolitical change? What did being German mean for them? Germany was, after all, for most people a cultural, linguistic, and romantic entity, more of a patriotic dream than a political reality. Neil MacGregor has forcefully reminded us of how novel anything like political unity was for twentieth-century Germans. Wolf Lepenies, in similar vein, has addressed the distaste for empirical politics among the cultural élite.[8] The patient and impatient compromises that are part and parcel of democratic practice were utterly foreign to them, indeed were seen as indications of weakness, and of decadent "civilization," compared with integrative German *Kultur*.

Probably still more difficult for us to grasp is what being Christian meant for ordinary Germans such as Lilo and Ernst during the war. How did they combine Christianity with their enthusiasm for National Socialism? Hitler, after all, had described Christianity as the systematic cultivation of human failure.[9] How did so many of his followers, including Ernst and Lilo, manage to convince themselves that their Christian faith and practice was compatible with National Socialist policies and ideals?

Ernst Sommer was born in September 1912, way up in the north of Germany, in the village of Wienboeken, in Schleswig-Holstein. His father, August, volunteered for the army in the First World War when Ernst was only four years old. August died in Rumanian captivity in 1916, and the family could never get to the bottom of what had happened to him. Ernst,

---

7. Lilo, on New Year's Eve 1940, follows up a passionate declaration of love to Ernst by saying she would be off to bed after listening to a broadcast by Goebbels.

8. MacGregor, *Germany: Memories of a Nation*; Lepenies, *The Seduction of Culture*.

9. Evans, *The Third Reich at War*, 547; cf. Evans, *The Third Reich in Power*, 220–60.

though only a four-year-old, vividly experienced the shock and distress of his mother when she heard the news. The blood totally drained from her face.[10] August had been a deacon in the Lutheran church, running the local orphanage, and then became overseer of a barracks for the workers on the Kiel Canal. His formidable wife, Frieda, was a committed Christian, and the children, including the two boys, Ernst and Hans, were brought up in a strict but warm Lutheran piety. Ernst's mother attended church in the morning on Sundays and went to a chapel gathering in the evenings. Her piety was combined with an unquestioning patriotism.

This tough, full-throated pride in Germany communicated itself to her children. Loyalty, courage, and honor were a mark of being German. The children's books of the period are full of boys in spotless army and naval uniforms, marching, drumming, and waving flags, of girls in nursing gear looking after the troops. Copies of Lilo's and Ernst's own books have survived, and through them we catch a glimpse of their own childhood. While still a baby, Lilo was given as a Christmas present in 1915 the children's picture book *Vater ist im Kriege (Daddy's off to War)*; the front page features the crown princess holding her baby; the signature of the crown prince is scrawled beneath one illustration; captions in verse accompany pictures of "our boys in blue," of sailors manning a gun, of soldiers in the trenches, of a field canteen bringing up goulash, of sharpshooters, of biplane pilots, of cavalrymen, submariners, and Christmas at the Front.[11]

It would be misleading, though, to suggest that all the books they read as children struck a militaristic note, as a well-thumbed edition of Hans Christian Andersen's fairy tales testifies. They grew up with typical children's books, and clearly began reading from a very early age. Lilo had read the touching "tales for our dear children": *Perlgückelchen und Weißmäuschen (Pearly Eyes and the Little White Mouse)*: naughty Pearly Eyes, alas, disobeyed her parents and so died an early death![12] Probably both of them had read the delightfully illustrated rhymes and naughty adventures, though all with a moral touch, of Heinrich Hoffmann's *Struwwelpeter (Shock-Headed*

---

10. Ernst to Lilo, February 18, 1936.

11. The book was a fund-raising enterprise for the war, sponsored by a group of patriotic German women, the *Kriegskinderspende deutscher Frauen*; Presber, *Vater ist im Kriege*; in 1919 another patriotic women's organization commissioned Bars, *Michel Hannemanns Traum (Dream)* for Germany's young people; its poems and pen-and-ink drawings feature soldiers marching into France and children piloting a warplane.

12. Georg, ed., *Andersens Schönste Märchen*; Hoffmann, *Der Struwwelpeter*; Niethammer, *Bei Gacks und Andere Geschichten*; Köhler, *Perlgückelchen und Weißmäuschen*.

Childhood, Youth, and Marriage

Peter); Ernst was given Vera Niethammer's *Bei Gacks und Andere Geschichten für Kleine Leute (Stories for Little People)* in 1919 as a Christmas present. Much more difficult to trace are the family stories they grew up with, or the prayers they said going to bed. This, of course, was a culture of the book, of the spoken and sung word, when even radios were a rarity.

The Sommer family struggled financially, but with support from generous church families, they managed. Ernst remembered it as a frugal time, with the catastrophic inflation of the early 1930s hitting them hard. It was quite a large family for his widowed mother to look after, with two girls, Leni and Tudi (Gertrud), and two boys. Hans was the youngest. The two brothers were good mates. Ernst was an enthusiastic pupil at school, learning English and French, enjoying sports, swimming, and singing. His restless energy could get him into all manner of scrapes, and into big trouble with his mother, who literally wielded the big stick on many occasions. He learned to play the violin and the recorder. He later remembered his childhood with affection and deep gratitude to his mother. He was a serious lad, who got on well with all his siblings. Leni, the eldest, comes across as intelligent and enterprising. She helped Ernst with his schoolwork. She had to leave school early to boost the family finances. She and Ernst were to remain close friends.[13]

In his Christmas letter of 1941 to his mother, Ernst looked back with pleasure on his childhood:

> *At Christmas I will be in meditative mood. In my thoughts I will be with my dear family and with you all in the home I know so well. You, dear mother, always made Christmas a quite special occasion, and throughout my life I draw upon that. You can imagine, I'm sure, how helpful it is for me to think of it when I'm at the Front! I wish you a happy, blessed Christmas with all my heart.*[14]

It does appear to have been a happy family, yet its values were traditional and circumscribed, and rather authoritarian. Youthful poverty hammered home for Ernst that life was struggle, and that only a strong will would enable one to triumph over adversity.

Their father's death would have cast its shadow. His mother, Frieda, was overcome with emotion when at the annual *Heldengedenktag* (the memorial service to the heroes of the World War), Ernst accompanied the

---

13. Ernst to Lilo, February 19, 1936.
14. Ernst to Lilo, December 8, 1941.

singing of the very emotional *ich hatt' einen Kamerad* (I lost my comrade) on his violin, the son honoring the father.[15]

Ernst was a good singer; his well-thumbed songbooks extol the loveliness of the rivers, hills, and forests, the meadows and fertile soil of Germany—the fatherland—and extol the soldierly virtues. He had a particular love for his own region, with its sometimes sandy soil and rough heather slopes, and its *Knicks* (raised boundaries to the fields), full of shrubs and birdlife. It demanded hard work and calloused hands, but he belonged there, and it belonged to him.[16] After school was over, he went on to train as a primary-school teacher, passing his initial exam at the end of March, 1933, just as Hitler came to power.

After six months in the Arbeitsdienst (Labor Service), in 1934 he participated with enthusiasm in the *Landjahr*, the National Socialist training program for students and those just out of school. This "year on the land" involved working on farms for long hours, taking part in paramilitary exercises, and the becoming inculcated with National Socialist ideals. Ernst looked back on this time with pleasure and was later to renew contact with the farming families he had lodged with. He was a very determined young man. His letter to Lilo in September 1935, a sort of self-portrait, is quite solemn, essay-like, tracing his emergence as his own person, grateful for heritage and parents, but making his own way in high school and university at Kiel. He talks of his East Frisian bloodstock, but also of firming up of his own personality. "What a person becomes, achieves, depends on his willpower." Honor, purity, and the tough struggle for *Wahrhaftigkeit* (inner integrity and authenticity) are key values for him. All this somewhat portentous language comes in a love letter, expressing the "fabulous clarity" he feels about his love for Lilo and the delight that she is drawn to him![17]

Perhaps it was around this time that he joined the *Sturmabteilung* (SA). He formally took the SA oath in April 1936. He could be mordantly critical of the incompetence and stupidity of some of the SA leaders in his local area, but he enjoyed the marching and the torchlight parades, and could spend four hours in the evening after work wandering from house to house on foot, collecting for the *Winterhilfswerk* (Winter Relief Organization), the National Socialist welfare program.[18] He also had a leader-

15. Gerda Sommer to Lilo, March 10, 1936.
16. Ernst to Lilo, January 4, 1935.
17. Ernst to Lilo, September 18, 1938.
18. Ernst to Lilo, January 26, 1936; the *Sturmbahnführer* (major) had marched the

Childhood, Youth, and Marriage

ship role with the local Hitler Youth group, groaning occasionally at the expectations, costly in time and money, that he participate in the regional parades of the *Bannaufmarsch*, the Hitler Youth. There are hints about *eine saumässige Verfassung* (the gross indifference) of some of the young folk to the National Socialist movement. They couldn't care less.

Ernst passed his final, practical exam in the little village school of Schalkholz with distinction in September 1937. His enthusiasm and quiet confidence as a teacher shone through. He was aware of the sensitivity of some of his pupils as well as the "inborn thickness" of some of them. He would take them out to the woods, get them to listen to the birdsong and identify the trees. He played his recorder so that the children could sing and dance together, a rather delightful picture.[19] His young pupils ate out of his hand. He had a strong sense of his calling to be a teacher, and knew he had good people skills. As he wrote four years later from the Russian Front: "I'm basically an optimist. I believe there is good in everyone. That is why I'm into education, body and soul. I need people around me. No one can succeed as a teacher unless they believe in the good in people."[20]

His success in passing this final exam moved the young teacher to tears. His letter to his fiancée, Lilo, describes every step in the process and his subsequent relief and elation:

> *It is all so strange. A few days ago I was under this huge pressure, normal, of course, for any conscientious person, and now I am so relieved and carefree! One is like a racing car which has been tearing along at 150 km an hour and has now suddenly braked to a total halt. Mentally you're still charging on and can hardly come to a stop. But very gradually one calms down. It's all over!*
>
> *I could scarcely believe it. Passed with distinction! Who would have believed it! In my wildest dreams I never dreamt of that! What do you think about your Ernst? Are you a bit proud of him? I'm happy if I can give you joy. Your part in the experience is what caps it all for me. Dear lass, if only you could hold my head in your hands now and drink in the sweet dreams of my love, my beloved one!*

---

men for miles in freezing weather without coats, while he sat muffled up in his car and made no provision for the men's food.

19. Ernst to Lilo, April 20, 1936; May 21, 1936.
20. As he wrote shortly before his death; Ernst to Lilo, December 16, 1941; . . . *ich bin nun einmal von Grund auf Optimist, halte jeden Menschen für gut und möchte allen Menschen Gutes tun. Deshalb bin ich auch mit Leib und Seele Pädagoge. Ich brauche Menschen zum Leben und wer nicht an das Gute im Menschen glaubt, kann kein Erzieher sein.*

Here's how it went: The exam began at 7.30 a.m. on Thursday 16 September. The kids arrived on time, or almost on time. I got them talking about the mill, about the work of the farmers, about how dismayed the farmers were when the storm left the corn-fields soaking wet. . . . The children were lively. It was fun. I then read out the poem, and that came off too. Arithmetic went like clockwork. I drilled them on local history and geography; a great success, with me stressing the pleasure it gives, the actual experience of the land, and how it makes one proud of one's origins. To finish off I played the recorder and sang a little. I emphasized the importance of giving the pupils a feel for the language. I was asked about the racial makeup of the children, their physical characteristics, and their spiritual qualities. I was happy to speak freely about that. It is tricky stuff, but I felt 100 percent at ease and could cope. [It is unclear what he understood by this, though he did state in December 1941 that: "Every person's destiny is determined by his genetic makeup."] *I noticed what a good impression it made on the examiners. It had become more of a conversation rather than an examination.*[21]

His idealism about his role as a teacher at this time is unmistakable: "Keep pure and aim at real maturity, that's my motto. God in one's heart, the world at one's feet, one's great mission in life: serving Germany! Together with you, it's as good as done."[22]

Ernst taught in the village school of Schalkholz but felt inhibited by the lack of any intellectual stimulation and the small-mindedness of the place, especially in the winter.[23] He tried to spend an hour a day practicing the violin, and after tea he and his brother, Hans, would chat with their mother, who kept house for them. The two brothers often sang together. Hans sometimes added a *Heil Hitler* to his letters, and his youthful zeal for the National Socialist cause is evident in his being chosen in 1936 for one of the *Schulungsburg* (special summer schools) for up-and-coming leaders.[24] By the time Hans had his tertiary education Nazi ideology had thoroughly

---

21. Ernst to Lilo, September 17, 1937; a school text belonging to him, however, *Küken Steigt ins Leben* is a cleverly illustrated introduction to National Socialist racialist ideology, emphasizing the importance of Aryan ancestry and ending with six pages on the criminal and corrupting influence of the Jews, and on the undue cost to society of genetically defective people.

22. Ernst to Lilo, September 17, 1937.

23. Ernst to Lilo, March 5, 1936.

24. Ernst to Lilo, July 12, 1936.

CHILDHOOD, YOUTH, AND MARRIAGE

penetrated the curriculum. Indeed his older brother was later worried that his absorption in Party gatherings meant that he neglected his studies.

In 1938 Ernst moved to be the head teacher at the village school in Wrohm. The daily routine there began at 8:00 a.m. with *Heil Hitler*, then a prayer and a hymn or a song. School finished at noon, but the early afternoon would often be taken up with singing, reading, gymnastics, and recorder playing. For his youngest pupils he used the attractive anthology *Tausend Sterne Leuchten (A Thousand Stars Are Shining)*, simple childlike poems with illustrations to suit; and for the older children *Tausendstimmiges Leben (Life in a Thousand Voices)*, traditional poems on the whole, some with a military theme.[25]

These villages, Schalkholz and Wrohm, were traditional farming communities, speaking *Plattdeutsch*, the lower German dialect, and proud of the yearly round of festivals, each boasting its singing group and its gymnastic club. The arrival of the storks in spring was a great event. Peat, coke (coal residue), and briquettes were used for heating and cooking; the roofs were covered with reeds or tiles. The winters could be bitterly cold. To a large extent it was a self-sufficient economy, which was a definite boon when food rationing took hold during the war. Each house had its garden, for everyone was reliant on their gardens for vegetables and for the fruit that was bottled or dried at harvesttime; many households had chicken coops and rabbit coops as well. Hardly any homes, though, boasted a telephone or a radio. The taxi was the only car in the village. There was never much money to spare. If you got sick, there was no money for a doctor—or only as a last resort.

When we turn to Lilo the comparison is sharp; she had anything but an easy childhood: her family was less strained financially, but her childhood was marred by bitter conflicts between her father and a mother who knew how to nurse her grievances. A very attractive woman, her mother was kept busy in kitchen and garden, but she showed little warmth to Lilo; her brother, Dieter, was the favorite. Lilo related well to her father, Paul Struck, who was the local primary school teacher and cantor in the church at Spantekow, in Pomerania, near the Baltic, with its six hundred inhabitants. He enjoyed considerable respect in the local community, both in and out of school, though Lilo knew of at least one extramarital relationship he had with an ex-pupil. She was proud of him. However, he overworked, and

---

25. Hirt, ed., *Tausend Sterne Leuchten*; *Tausendstimmiges Leben*; other educational books included Simrock, ed., *Reineke Fuchs*; he had two editions of this.

was tense at times, indeed on the edge of a complete breakdown. On one occasion she hid his revolver, fearing that he would take his own life. He smashed a window on another occasion in his anger. It was intolerable for Lilo to be caught between her warring parents.[26]

Music was an early love. She played the piano, the organ, the recorder, and the lute. One of her songbooks, *Das aufrecht Fähnlein (The Flag Held High)* gives us an indication of the broad palette of religious hymns, patriotic songs, ballads, children's songs, and folk songs she grew up with.[27] She was on good terms with her brother, Dieter. To escape the poisonous atmosphere at home, though, she had to leave Spantekow for the coastal town of Swinemünde, where her Aunt Lisbeth lived. Lisbeth's husband, Arthur Friedrich, taught in the lyceum, or secondary school, that she attended. However, like many girls at the time she did not get the chance to stay at school long enough to get the *Abitur* (university entrance), which was the gateway to university and the professions. Ernst did have the *Abitur*, and she was to struggle with a sense of inferiority to him as a result.

Paul Struck was a Party member, and it may have been through his influence that the nineteen-year-old Lilo got the chance to train as a leader of the Landjahr in 1934–1935. She appears in photos from that time in the uniform of the *Bund Deutscher Mädel* (the National Socialist young women's group) as an attractive, sporty young woman. The Landjahr opened up new worlds for her. One senses, as with Ernst, her idealism about the emergent new Germany. She notes explicitly that her involvement in the Labor Service and the Landjahr stemmed from this idealism.[28]

She and Ernst first met in the summer of 1935 in the Schleswig-Holstein town of Burg, where she was one of the leaders of the Landjahr program, living in the attractive old residence, *Haus Sonnenschein*. Ernst had arrived in Burg with a young men's group. Burg, with its three thousand inhabitants, was Ernst's hometown, and he was deeply attached to it. He found out that the attractive young woman who had caught his eye played the organ in the local church and tracked her down there. From the beginning, it seems (for all her natural shyness) that they fell headlong and rapturously in love. It may have helped that she too was, so happy in Burg.

Her warmth and naturalness meant that she enjoyed her role as a leader of the groups of young women, as they worked on the land, sang

26. Lilo to Ernst, August 1, 1936.
27. Henssel, ed., *Das Aufrecht Fähnlein*.
28. Lilo to Ernst, March 7, 1936.

Childhood, Youth, and Marriage

their hearts out, and dreamt of a better future for Germany. Or that was the theory! In reality, many were city kids, homesick and unsure of themselves at first. Motivating them could be hard work. The girls from Westphalia and from the Saarland were often spoiled and lazy, full of unreal expectations, she complained, unlike the hardworking ones from Schleswig. Perhaps, she speculated, the French occupation, which had just ended after the 1935 referendum in the Saar, had demoralized them. Some, too, seemed of mixed race, with thick lips and frizzy hair. National Socialist propaganda spoke of mixed race children as "Rhineland bastards." Lilo talks of working very long hours, preparing the daily two hours of teaching, sometimes going on night marches, and leading them in sports and swimming.[29] A high point was an excursion to Kiel where her group joined two thousand others. The hushed attentiveness of the young women as they listened to the rhetoric from the platform impressed her.[30] She threw herself into the work, and bonded well with the girls, but was often worn out.

Initially there was considerable latitude in the programs, and church attendance could be fitted in. In Burg her girls actually joined the church choir, and Lilo herself struck up a friendship with the church organist. There is a fascinating account in one of the letters of the girls' excitement as Christmas approached, humming the carols in the dormitory to the accompaniment of a mouth organ. Singing brought to life all the memories of past Christmases, of Mary, Joseph, and the Christ child. You could express in song what was difficult to say in words. "Singing, playing the recorder, the lute and the violin are part of camp life. We will never forget singing our Advent songs together, the last activity in our camp before we go back home to sing carols beside the candles on the Christmas tree."[31] National Socialist ideals and Christian themes are here closely interwoven.

Lilo's down-to-earth approach made her sharply critical of the exaggerated romanticism that surfaced at a leadership course on the Baltic in August 1935. She had loved the camping and swimming in the Baltic, but didn't mince her words in her report to her friend and future husband, Herr Sommer:

---

29. Lilo to her parents, May 25, 1935; one wonders if different religious and political backgrounds might be in play here; in the Rhineland and the Saar Catholicism and social democratic traditions were stronger than in Schleswig-Holstein.

30. Lilo to Ernst, October 3, 1935.

31. This document, which was filed together with her 1935 letters, is not signed or dated, but its language suggests that it originated with Lilo.

> *The last eight days were so packed with events and so utterly ghastly, that we want to put them right out of our minds. In a word, you were expected to leave your brain behind, and go primitive. The emphasis on experience is all very well, but became totally bizarre when it is so forced and unreal. You can't spend a whole week chanting slogans and singing about being the seed for the future, walking barefoot upon the sacred soil, gazing into the sunset with enraptured eyes. Let them think if they like that one is superficial, too intellectual, out of touch with one's instincts. To avoid being impolite one had to pretend enthusiasm and act as if one was carried away by it all, but I felt a total hypocrite.*[32]

A remarkable, moving letter mirrors her confusion as she comes to terms with Ernst's wooing of her. She asks for time to think things through. In the hectic round of her daily work with the girls it was hard to find space for the contemplation, peace, and quietness she needed. "I am so dissatisfied with myself, so lacking in self-confidence." In reality she coped with every challenge well, wedding careful preparation with enthusiasm, but deep down she feared she was a fraud, a dilettante. She felt *zersplittert* (torn apart) between her attraction to him and an "almost holy reticence." She knew it stemmed from the unhappy marriage of her parents, which had marked her earliest childhood memories with such unspeakable sadness and *unmenschlichen Schmerzen* (inhuman suffering). "There it is, my dear, I've opened up my soul to you."[33]

His thoughtful and caring responses gradually overcame her hesitations. He promised to help her get over her emotional scars from the past, and counseled her not to let herself be stressed out with the work. Space and time are undergirded by eternity. There was no point rushing around and sitting up to all hours. There was more to life than the *Landjahr*. Peace and freedom come from doing one's duty as best one can but leaving the rest to God, the *Allvater* (Father of all).[34]

Yet it was, despite his rather preachy advice, as she put it, anything but a one-sided relationship. "You are mine. I am thine," they said to one another, quoting an anonymous medieval German poet. She had no intention of being bossed around by "her dear big boy," though highly appreciative of his thoughtfulness, and aware that in his presence apparently insuperable

---

32. All this in a letter to "Herr Sommer," her future husband; August 26, 1935; cf. Leppien and Leppien, *Mädel-Landjahr in Schleswig-Holstein*.

33. Lilo to Ernst, September 19, 1935.

34. Ernst to Lilo, September 23, 1935.

difficulties were put into perspective. She ridiculed his jealousy about an evening dance she had participated in. What utter nonsense! She had no time for such prudery and successfully rode out his indignation after she had swept aside his objections.[35] He took things too seriously at times, she commented, reminding him that all of us live with a tension between our ideals and daily reality.

She knew her own mind, ran a tight ship in the hostel, and was unperturbed, for example, by the imminent visit of a phalanx of two hundred girls. She steered her life by her own moral compass. The heartlessness, for example, of *Landjahr* leaders like Frau Hagemann to the death of one of her young colleagues, and to the illnesses of others (including herself) appalled her. She could not abide their coarse, immodest talk, either.[36]

She had nothing but contempt, either, for a German Labor Front speaker who did not connect with her girls but droned on in an arrogant, self-satisfied way. Yet she swallowed whole the Nazi mythology about the so-called heroes of Langemark, where in fact masses of young infantrymen had died in a futile assault in 1914.[37] Her father had been recently installed as the leader of the returned soldiers association in the district, and she was proud of his natural gifts as a speaker and of his engagement with them and the whole community for the sake of the fatherland. There is a reference to tensions about the association, which was regarded by some as reactionary. Presumably the reference is to National Socialist suspicion of traditional military values. Lilo spoke warmly of the film shown on the occasion of her father's appointment, *Im gleichen Schritt und Tritt (Marching in Step)*, in which Hitler presides over the glorification of the First World War, with mass singing of "Ich hatt' einen Kameraden" ("I Had a Comrade"). It was the National Socialist death cult at its most overt.[38] Watching it today online one shudders.

By September 1935 the formal greeting to "Herr Sommer" had been replaced by "my dearest Ernst." The letters flew between them, and were read again and again. They exchanged favorite songs, wanted to play Haydn and Mozart together—he on the violin, she on the piano. Their separation,

35. Lilo to Ernst, November 27, 1935.

36. Lilo to Ernst, September 25, 1935.

37. . . . *furchtbar von sich eingenommen und arrogant;* Lilo to Ernst, November 11, 1935.

38. Lilo to Ernst, February 23, 1935; the film can be accessed on YouTube and makes for grim viewing.

as she returned to Pomerania, drove them crazy; they could scarcely bear it, while their times of togetherness were like a fairy tale in their happiness.[39] Lilo felt transformed; she was becoming a new person whom she did not recognize, and was just bursting with love. The words of his letters were like the caress of his hands. "I do believe your love makes me good and reverent."[40] Her spontaneity complemented his reflective and more logical approach, as both acknowledged. He focused on the facities of life, the *was*, she on its emotional dimension, the *wie*.[41]

She traveled to Schalkholz, the little village in which he was teaching, to spend Christmas with him in 1935, staying with family friends of the Sommers in Burg. In no time they were engaged to be married. Lilo's family was delighted, her father being thrilled that Ernst, too, was a teacher, and that his brother, Hans, was enrolled for Teacher's College. Two teaching families were coming together. He wrote Ernst a very cordial letter, with an account of his own views on teaching. He enjoyed history teaching most; aspects of racial biology still puzzled him.[42] Lilo felt her "little heart" would burst with so much happiness.[43]

Almost from the beginning their personal history has to be set against convulsive political change. Shortly after their engagement, the German army marched into the Rhineland in March 1936. Lilo was beside herself with joy:

> *Our marvelous* Führer! Indescribable to *witness the jubilation of the population at the advance into the Rhineland, the music of the military bands, the applause in the Reichstag. And now a torchlight procession this very evening! How I would love, my dear, to be part of it, to be swept along by the jubilation of the people. I'd love too, to see our Land Year girls in Saarbrücken, who'll be experiencing the German army for the first time.*

Germany, she felt, was on equal terms at last, free from the Versailles Treaty. How great to be able to participate in this historic event through the radio.[44]

She was equally enthusiastic about Hitler's "wonderful" speech about marriage and motherhood, delivered in Nuremberg to the National

39. Ernst to Lilo, October 27, 1935.
40. Ernst to Lilo, November 5, 1935.
41. Ernst to Lilo, October 11, 1937.
42. Paul Struck to Ernst, February 23, 1936.
43. Lilo to Ernst, November 8, 1935.
44. Lilo to Ernst, June 3, 1936.

Socialist women's movement, "He spoke with such deep respect to the heart of every woman," she wrote to Ernst. Lying on the couch in the dark with a friend she had listened to every word and been profoundly stirred, thinking of her own relationship to Ernst, so *hoch und rein* (pure and exalted), as the Führer had put it in such tender terms. The two of them, Ernst and herself, also wanted of course to start a family. "God willing, I will bear children for you and for our nation." She so looks forward to this. "We two, you and me, will be at one in our child." It made her giddy just to think about it.[45]

But after their engagement they had to wait two long years before a wedding could be contemplated. Ernst's mother, Frieda, who kept house for him at Schalkholz, was not convinced that Lilo was good enough for her beloved Ernst, and put numerous obstacles in her way, including her having to take full-time courses in cooking, sewing, gardening and other housework! She also insisted that before he embarked on marriage, Ernst give priority to providing financial assistance to his brother, Hans, who was still completing his tertiary study.[46] She even wrote to Lilo's parents and to her aunt Martha in Swinemünde, urging them to support her in delaying the marriage.

Lilo, however, was a mature young woman who had more than proved her competence in her two years with the *Landjahr*, rising to be a *Schar-Führer* (a fully qualified leader). Her future mother-in-law's demands were absurd and unfair, but for the sake of peace Lilo reluctantly complied with them in 1936 and then into 1937. She understandably felt bitter and resentful about these pressures, and it spilled over into her relationship with Ernst, who was very loyal to his mother and tried to play the mediator for a while. But the conditions he set for Lilo, including understanding for his mother, seemed to her very harsh, and drove her to the edge of despair. She angrily wrote him that she apparently came second to her mother in his affections.[47]

45. Lilo to Ernst, May 13, 1936.

46. Ernst tried to play the mediator, an unenviable role, especially since he himself had a very traditionalist view of the woman's place in society; in the end he pled with Lilo not to speak disrespectfully of his mother, and to address any concerns directly to her and not to use him as an intermediary; both women felt, in his view, that the other looked down on the other; they should, he thought, try taking things more casually, show more *Schnurzigkeit* (detachment); Ernst, November 24, 1939; although relations improved, Lilo always felt a lack of warmth toward herself from her mother-in-law; when she was down with a severe chill in February 1941, Ernst's mother left her in the lurch; Lilo to Ernst, February 7, 1941.

47. Lilo to Ernst, February 4, 1937.

The waiting seemed endless to her, not least at a time when premarital relations were taboo. And there seemed no guarantee that another demand would not follow from Ernst's mother. The housework Lilo was being forced into had nothing creative about it for her, and its pointlessness, when they could already be happily married, made her feel "as if everything in me is dead."[48] He had his teaching to stimulate and stretch him, and she felt that he totally failed to appreciate the effect of the separation on her. She was aware that she might be oversensitive, but he, on the other hand, could too easily brush her worries aside with his more logical approach. Both of them wondered at times if the marriage could actually go ahead. After a particularly torrid exchange of letters in which Lilo again criticized his mother, he posed the question whether she was importing the dysfunctional relations from her family into his own.[49]

By October 1937 Lilo had had enough. In a letter that pulled out every stop, she gave Ernst an ultimatum. Whatever his mother thought, they must get married at once.[50] Deeply respectful of his mother as he was, Ernst capitulated, and told his sister, Leni, very firmly: "I am utterly committed to Lilo now and have no time at all for this rejection of her. . . . My whole future life belongs to her."[51] It was certainly a tumultuous relationship, the highs being as extreme as the lows. Minutes became eternities for both of them when they had to part after he visited her in August 1937.[52]

Ernst's military training in the reserve army began in October 1937 in Kolberg, in distant Pomerania. Affectionate letters flew between them, as they looked forward to having Christmas together in Spantekow. They lived for one another's letters, and he appreciated the cakes she sent him through the post.[53] But the long wait for the marriage, and the uncertainty about how his family felt about her, plunged her into depression, and in their exaggerations and undue anxiety her letters reflect this, provoking deep worry on Ernst's part. She seemed to have lost confidence in him.[54] Both of them were working long hours, and exhaustion—and writing letters very

48. Lilo to Ernst, October 12, 1936.
49. Ernst to Lilo, June 7, 1937.
50. Lilo to Ernst, October 31, 1937.
51. Ernst to Leni, December 6, 1937.
52. Ernst to Lilo, August 18, 1937.
53. Ernst to Lilo, November 7, 1937; January 30, 1937; his commanding officer picked him out as *Reserveoffiziersanwärter* (officer material).
54. Ernst to Lilo, November 25, 1937.

Childhood, Youth, and Marriage

late at night—no doubt played a role in the misunderstandings. Lilo was run ragged, lost weight, did not sleep. However, when he traveled to her parents' home in Spantekow to spend Christmas with her in December, the much anticipated visit was an incredibly successful one. Lilo wrote shortly after he had left: "I am so unbelievably happy when I think of you, and your postcard tells me that the same is true for you. Never before have I begun a new year with such confidence. . . . I lay in bed, my eyes wide open, and thought of you."[55]

The months immediately preceding the marriage in March, however, were extremely difficult and tense. Lilo was living at home in Spantekow, witnessing every day the unedifying tensions between her parents, frittering away her time at the demeaning tasks imposed on her by Ernst's mother, and working at the quite complicated financial and travel arrangements for a wedding that involved bringing Ernst's reluctant relatives from the northwest of Germany to distant Pomerania in the east, and finding accommodation for them. German bureaucracy required all manner of documentation. She and Ernst also had to plan the setting up of their future home in Wrohm. For a while it seemed that Lilo had to contemplate sharing the household with Ernst's mother. Money was a constant problem, and arranging a loan to finance initial household purchases took time. Lilo made some pocket money by working in a local office, which Ernst found demeaning. Women should work at home, not in offices, was his paternalist view.

Ernst himself was in the midst of negotiating his transfer from Schalkholz to the school at Wrohm and was frantically busy. All these decisions had to be agreed upon between the young couple by letter, and Lilo's epistles took on an increasingly hysterical tone. The confident young leader in Burg was no longer recognizable. She seemed close to a nervous breakdown, and Ernst's patience was stretched to breaking point.[56] Strong undercurrents of tension were to remain between Lilo and her future mother-in-law.

The marriage eventually took place in Lilo's parents' home in Spantekow on March 11, 1938, and appears to have gone off without a hitch. First the registrar's office, then the service in the church, leading on to the ensuing meal. Lilo had feared that Ernst's mother would make a scene at the

---

55. Lilo to Ernst, February 1, 1938.

56. To solve the acute accommodation problem, she had even suggested that they sleep separately on their wedding night. At that he put in an emphatic veto!

wedding, but nothing of the sort happened. It was to develop into a quite unusually rich marriage of heart and mind, body and soul.

The very next day after the wedding German troops marched into Austria, Hitler having ruthlessly railroaded the weak Austrian government into compliance, although majority support in the country had always favored independence. By the end of September this had been followed by the Munich Agreement, Hitler exploiting the hesitations and illusions of Britain and France, and the shortsightedness of Poland to march unopposed into what came to be known as the Sudetenland, the well-fortified western area of Czechoslovakia, with its high proportion of German speakers. To most Germans, including our young couple, the disarray of the Western powers contrasted with the flair of a Führer who knew precisely what he was doing, and possessed the means to achieve it. Already, though few knew this, he was planning an attack on France and Britain. In *Mein Kampf*, a book that was to be found by now in countless German homes, though probably read as little as the Bible, he had made crystal clear his intention to win for the Reich *Lebensraum*, territory in the east for German settlement. For all with eyes to see, it was obvious that the invasion of Poland would be next on the list. Thus the beginning of Ernst and Lilo's marriage coincided with the apparently unstoppable triumphal march of Hitler's diplomacy, backed by the rapid militarization of the economy. Their dreams of a happy life together appeared to jell with a new and glorious future for the new Germany.

There are hints, though, that relations between the young married couple could be stormy. At times she resisted his amorous advances.[57] Ernst talked of this early period as a sort of *Kampf* (struggle). They both wanted to be one in the fullest sense, physically and spiritually, but it was a fiery affair. Ernst understood, however, that they could not race into this new relationship, but had to take it step by step. As he saw it, their love was mutually enhancing, with a thousand different aspects to it. Each was now part of the other, and the children to come of the marriage would be their common legacy. She had become "an inexhaustible source of energy for my life here on earth." When troubles came, she should hold on to their love and to God's almighty power, and she would find the strength to endure anything.[58]

---

57. Lilo to Ernst, January 5, 1941.
58. Ernst to Lilo, November 25, 1939.

Childhood, Youth, and Marriage

Lilo talked later of how she dealt with these "initial marriage strains."[59] She would say to herself, "Stop that now, go to Ernst; as the woman you have to make the first move. And you never turned me away, my dearest.... My soul lies open before you, and in ever new ways I offer it up to you." So they kissed and made peace. The bond between them, as both stressed repeatedly, was one of mind and will, of heart and soul. In its purity and depth they felt that their love for one another was unparalleled. Lilo was determined to create a good home for herself, her husband, and their future children. Every fiber within her longed for him. "I am going to create a happy life for myself."[60]

The shadow of her own unhappy childhood spurred her on. Both relished the outdoors and sports (though Lilo had not the least interest in football [soccer]!) and had good social skills. Ernst's calm temperament is frequently referred to, as it put people at ease. They also brought a strong cultural inheritance into the union; they loved singing, played various instruments, had an appreciation for classical and folk music, and read widely in the German classics. Their poetry books are heavily annotated. Lilo had a formidable memory for songs, poems, fables, and fairy tales. Ernst rather fancied himself as an amateur philosopher.

Money was always tight in the young couple's household, but Lilo proved a good manager. She made do, drew up careful lists of priorities. Socks were darned, clothes sewn up from discarded garments. She hated running up debts, and cautioned Ernst about giving out too much money.

We can picture quite accurately their day-to-day life in Wrohm, as their marriage got underway. The world of the village was a tidy one. Appearances had to be kept up. The gravel fronting the street would be carefully raked each weekend. Patterns of relationships, the work on the land, and ideas and customs remained traditional. It was a peasant society. Lilo had already experienced in Burg the resistance of these small farmers to any challenge to their ways. They defended their own patch. They had an inborn suspicion of outsiders and of interference from the state. The teacher's house stood somewhat apart.[61] Here "proper German" was spoken, a degree of distance was kept, and a certain deference shown. Lilo

---

59. *Erstlingskrankheiten einer Ehe*; Lilo to Ernst, 5.6.41; there are hints of them in various letters, e.g. Ernst to Lilo, October 19, 1939; October 21, 1939.

60. *Ich will mir ein Glück bauen*; Lilo to Ernst, April 23, 1941.

61. An undated memo records an estimate for the refurnishing of the house: dining room with piano and typewriter, and a wardrobe in the hall, with most expense for the Herrenzimmer (the "best room"). Ernst to Lilo, November 11, 1939.

would play the piano for the singing at social gatherings. There are hints that some villagers felt the Sommers were too aloof. When in March 1941 rumors circulated that Ernst would be transferred out of the army to a large "Hitler school," the progressive *Aufbauschule* (intensive school) in Burg being mentioned, old Frau Grönhoff apparently muttered about the Sommers: "We scarcely know them anyway. They never appear, and keep to themselves."[62]

There are frequent references, though, to Ernst's popularity as a teacher. He led the Hitler Youth group in the village, as we have seen, and his brief trips to Belgium, Holland, and Denmark in 1938 would have been in connection with this.[63] One of the books in his possession was *Blut und Ehre (Blood and Honor)*, the songbook of the Hitler Youth, edited by Baldur von Schirach, the Reich Führer of the Hitler Youth. The book flew under the motto "The flag is greater than death." Certainly the themes of death and glory were all-pervasive, astonishingly so for our sensibilities today. These young National Socialists were envisaged marching side by side into a better future for the *Volk* (people), ready for any sacrifice. Traditional patriotic songs sat side by side with new National Socialist lyrics. Comradeship and a romantic love of nature are evoked by the stirring melodies. Ernst's battered copy testifies to its frequent use.[64] One wonders what the parents of his young followers, gathered round for endless games of cards in the winter, made of all this. The term *stur* (stolid) is often used for these Dithmarsch peasants. They were canny, cautious, and gave little away.

Ernst did manage to get back from training camp for the birth of their first child, Heinke, in February 1939. Lilo vividly remembered two years later their excitement during her pregnancy, the walks they took together, his solicitude for her, and his initial surprise and shock when she took his hand and placed it on the child kicking in the womb.[65] And then the birth came, four weeks premature:

> *I remember every tiny detail. How I woke you far too early at 2.30 a.m., for we were both so silly and inexperienced. Then at 7.30 you*

---

62. Lilo to Ernst, March 25, 1941.
63. Ernst to Lilo, April 8, 1939.
64. Von Schirach, ed., *Blut und Ehre*; other songbooks in his possession, such as Jöde, ed., *Der Musikant*; and Neuendorff, ed., *Volker Liederbuch* offer a wide range of folk songs, with the usual themes of love, the seasons of the year, festivals, wandering through the countryside, as well as patriotic and soldierly material.
65. Lilo to Ernst, January 28, 1941.

Childhood, Youth, and Marriage

> went to Buhmann for the taxi. *There followed four hours of waiting, patience, and still more patience. At 1.30 Dr Meier arrived and sat with you and Frau Schlüter* [the midwife]. *I can see you in your dark suit at the top of the bed. I don't remember particularly severe pain. Then you lifted me from the bed and put me on the kitchen table, and before I knew it, something was on my nose and I had to breathe in deeply. Bells were ringing in my ears and I heard everything through a fog. You seemed so far away, though I could hear your voices quite clearly. I managed to say, 'Don't start anything yet, I know what's happening.' That was the last thing I remembered. I woke up from far, far away, was in my own bed again, opened my eyes, and wanted to sit up. 'Keep still,' someone cried, and then I heard a baby croaking, saw Frau Gudewehr, Schlüter and Sister Magda busying themselves round the table. 'Frau Sommer. You have a little girl.' I can still hear how that sounded. 'Is she healthy?' I asked. You were sitting in the dining room with Dr Meier, drinking coffee, and came over to me at once and asked how I was feeling. I felt great. Now our little Sunday lass was there, our Heinke!*

The medical complications after the birth, including a kidney infection, proved painful, and she remembered how supportive Ernst was at that time, as nurse and comrade, nappying and feeding the baby. "How I love you . . . ," she wrote, as she recalled it all.[66]

Ernst loved hearing every little detail about his daughter's progress. He also sent his dirty clothes back to Wrohm to be washed! But his main concern was for his wife, now pregnant with their second child. Scarlet fever put the camp into quarantine in January 1940 and made leave impossible. "I explained the position to the lieutenant: sick child, heating not working, pipes frozen, lack of coal, wife pregnant," and he hoped that the quarantine could soon be lifted so he could get home over the weekend.[67] His visit in May ended with some tension between them, but he soon apologized to her for his temperamental outburst; apparently she had been accusing him of indifference to her domestic troubles.[68] They were settling down, though, as a married couple, and the children were beginning to appear.

---

66. Lilo to Ernst, January 28, 1941.
67. Ernst to Lilo, January 17, 1940.
68. Ernst to Lilo, May 3, 1940; May 6, 1940.

2

The False Sense of Peace

All will be well. All will be well. All manner of things will be well.
—JULIAN OF NORWICH, FOURTEENTH CENTURY

As early as 1937 Ernst had volunteered to enroll in the reserve army, which throws a light on the strength of his commitment to National Socialist policies; Lilo had encouraged the decision, partly for patriotic reasons, but she was aware, too, that joining the army reserve would also prop up their finances. Despite the memories of the carnage of the First World War, including his own father's wretched death, Ernst was delighted to be able at last to wear the uniform of the German army. He felt that they had learned to put personal wishes aside, for behind everything stands Germany, and this thought should energize them. He had always been a doer. The meaning of life, as he frequently expressed it, was "in work, in struggle, in commitment."[1] In National Socialist Germany this meant commitment to the armed forces.

Ernst was called up for active service in July 1939. From now on his school duties were at an end, but while he was still in training he was able to get home on leave fairly often. He loved flicking through the photo album Lilo had sent. He was disappointed that he couldn't make it for her birthday on August 4, 1939, but was glad to turn up as the proud father at Heinke's baptism shortly afterwards:

---

1. Ernst to Lilo, February 18, 1937.

The False Sense of Peace

My little one!

As so often things have turned out differently from what we'd planned. I was on guard duty on Sunday and couldn't leave the barracks. Today was the oath-taking ceremony. I did a swap with a comrade who was on duty today and this gives me time to write to you without any distractions and to congratulate you on your birthday.

So I wish you most heartily all strength and good health for the year ahead. I will continue to stand beside you as the loyal comrade in your life and help you as you help me. When one is in the army one learns how little loyalty to one's partner tends to mean. But you can rely on me. It is sad that I can't be with you on the fourth. But I still think I can be with you for a quiet hour on the Saturday.

Father will, I'm sure, be setting up the birthday table for you. Please excuse it if the presents don't all arrive at the same time. In this parcel are two lanterns for the occasion. Let's hope we can still experience a nice evening amidst your flickering candles. I'm so pleased at the piles of sweet things that will be sure to be there. I know your weakness for such delicacies.

I'm just off the telephone. The dress is being dyed blue, and I'll bring it with me on Saturday.

Should I bring a scarf or buttons or anything else? I fear it's too late for that. My little one, if all else fails, then take the half-past-one car and we'll buy something together. You should look your best for the baptism [of Heinke]. Can you bring me 10 Mark? As I said, I'd love it if you could come on Saturday. But with all the preparations you may not make it. Will you be with the Schlotfeldts and Mother for lunch? It's all arranged with the pastor, isn't it? All my love, Ernst.[2]

Hans, Ernst's brother, and Hans-Dieter, Lilo's brother, were also conscripted. Ernst's initial officer training took place in nearby Heide, then in Lübeck. He couldn't be bothered with all the military drills: standing to attention, waiting for an order, breaking into a run, and being ordered about. It left no time at all for reflection. Ernst was critical, too, of some of his fellows, who seemed more interested in drink and women than anything else. He was part of a nation actively preparing for war, but like most Germans assumed that, as had been the case with the Rhineland, Austria, and the Sudetenland, France and Britain would not see it in their interests to challenge the Reich. It would not come to war. Hitler's masterly diplomacy, backed by Germany's military strength, would win out again. In April Britain, France,

---

2. Ernst to Lilo, August 2, 1939.

and Russia had agreed to support Poland if it were invaded, but the nonaggression pact with Stalin on August 23, 1939, which envisaged the partition of Poland between the Reich and Russia, bolstered the conviction that the Western powers would not intervene. Ernst, writing from his army training in Heide, was supremely confident that it would not come to war, though Poland would *seinen Lohn haben* (get what it deserved).[3]

Lilo was more worried, and sensed by the beginning of September 1939 that things were moving to a crisis. She had no radio of her own yet, but after hearing the Führer's speech she concluded, "Now things will take their course." She could only pray and hope for the best as far as Ernst was concerned. In his absence she found herself doing jobs she had never tackled before—taking an axe, for example, to knock the stopper out of the water cask that needed cleaning. She was distressed to see how badly the school at Wrohm was faring under its replacement teacher. She and Ernst planned various visits on leave from Lübeck and then in 1940 from Potsdam.[4]

Like many, probably most Germans Lilo had been thrilled by Hitler's foreign policy successes, but was anything but happy at the outbreak of war. She saw everything now with the eyes of a mother and a wife. The declaration of war by France and England immediately after the invasion of Poland on September 1, 1939, was a cruel shock. Even at this early date Lilo began to contemplate the possibility that she might have to live on without Ernst. War, she knew, would cost the country millions of Reichsmark, and although the German losses in Poland of ten thousand men were minor compared with those of the Poles, it still made her shudder. The Führer's speech had given her no comfort because she was conscious of the heavy sacrifices ahead.[5] Before the end of the month, however, the brave resistance of Poland had come to an end, overrun in a highly mobile *Blitzkrieg* by the Reich's two thousand tanks and its overwhelming air power. The Russian army, meanwhile, surged into eastern Poland.

In November she took the train for a surprise visit to Spantekow in Pomerania for her father's birthday, which proved a huge success.[6] Ernst had advised her against it, not only thinking of her pregnancy, but also making dark hints about military movements that might hinder her re-

---

3. Ernst to Lilo, August 23, 1939.
4. Lilo to Ernst, September 1, 1939; September 4, 1939.
5. Lilo to Ernst, October 8, 1939.
6. Lilo to Ernst, November 5, 1939.

turn. However he was full of enthusiasm and admiration for her grit in undertaking the journey.[7] Soon they were eagerly planning her travel to Lübeck over the weekend, very much a young couple in love. She described to him her "golden" little toddler, clapping her hands in her blue dress while her mother sang for her. She wished Ernst were there to see it.

He wrote to Lilo on 30 November, the day Soviet troops marched into Finland, from "Adolf's Heights," a training camp near Münster. It was bucketing down rain, but after his experiences in the Labor Service, the Land Year, and the Hitler Youth expeditions he had led, nothing rattled Ernst. The mood of his comrades, he enthused, was excellent.[8] No wonder. Germany seemed to be carrying everything before it. Their mood would have been even better had they known that the stubborn resistance of the Finns would vitiate the poorly planned Russian campaign.

After the blitzkrieg in Poland there were no substantial military actions on the ground in the west despite the overwhelming predominance of Allied forces over the German ones at the time. A so-called phony war dragged on, Lilo found the uncertainty hard to take:

> *This weird stalemate will gave way soon to decisive action. My Ernst, what does fate hold for us? On the great scale of things the fate of individuals is insignificant, but for that individual a whole world of peace and happiness can collapse and the next moment suffering and distress take over. This struggle against England is for both nations a life and death affair, and will cost us endless sacrifices.*[9]

Ernst's response was to ask why she was so down in the mouth, almost fatalistic. One had to trust in God, and in the *hohe Güter* (higher values). She should face the future with confidence for his sake, for that of the children, and for that of the nation. These tensions between the wife at home and the husband having to gear up psychologically for war were widespread and were soon to become a concern of the Gestapo.[10] Ernst

---

7. Ernst to Lilo, October 30, 1939; an unusual feature of this letter is that Ernst admits to being exhausted, after vigorous training and long rides on his horse, Prince, through the countryside. He loved horseback riding and waxed lyrical about the autumn colors of the woods he rode through; Ernst to Lilo, November 7, 1939; at times, though, he almost froze to death during winter rides on his horse, his bones feeling as though they would snap when he dismounted; Ernst to Lilo, February 19, 1940.

8. Ernst to Lilo, November 30, 1939.

9. Lilo to Ernst, November 5, 1939.

10. Ernst to Lilo, January 9, 1940; cf. Evans, *The Third Reich at War*, 543.

had a traditional concept of manly virtues: "We men belong at the Front."[11] There is no doubt, however, that he longed for the war to end quickly so he could be back with his beloved wife and his children. He had sensitivity and empathy for Lilo and could not hear enough about his little daughter.

As Advent got underway in 1939, Lilo found it difficult to get into an anticipatory mood. The outbreak of war had brought with it such uncertainty about the future. "War is the worst thing ever on earth." So many men would never return. She felt an inner sadness, and was unsure if Ernst would make it home for Christmas. It would be easier for him to cope with the separation, anyway, because of the company of others in training like him.[12] She kept herself busy knitting socks for little Heinke, who had a heavy cold, choking on the mucus, but Lilo was relieved when Dr. Meier assured her it was not whooping cough, and that Heinke's general health was excellent. "The news of the death of a Sp[antekow] schoolmate in Poland has been preying on me. Wrohm, too, has a casualty, the son of Sobronitzky. Klaußen (Mühle) lies in a Berlin field hospital with a fracture in his thigh, after ten days as a prisoner. Frahm has been discharged, as has Erwin, because of stomach ulcers."[13] The casualties from the Polish campaign were very much on her mind. To her great relief, however, Ernst did get leave and they could celebrate Christmas together. She wrote him, back in training camp again, on New Year's Eve, their last happy evening together vivid in her mind:

> *My beloved Ernst,*
>
> *Now the old year is fading. New Year's Eve always has a quite special memory for me: our engagement! You dear, good Ernst, I had never thought it could be so wonderful to be your wife. I know that there are so few men who are what you are. I am so proud of you, and infinitely grateful for the wealth and the love which have come into my life through you. Everything I have become in the years of our marriage I owe to you. It is a great, infinite happiness to be able to go through life at your side. I often ask myself, how have I deserved such a marvelous husband? It is an unmerited happiness and therefore I am so often fearful for our future, for your life. God has brought us together, and blessed our marriage, has gifted us Heinkele and a second new life. I look forward to the New Year with a warm*

---

11. Ernst to Lilo, May 29, 1940.
12. Lilo to Ernst, December 1, 1939.
13. Lilo to Ernst, September 25, 1939.

> *heart and pray to God to return you safely to me and the children. So I wanted to write to you today, to listen to Goebbels, and then head off to bed....*[14]

Letters and parcels flowed between them almost every second day.

By early 1940 she was heavily pregnant with her second child. At times, especially when Heinke was sick, she found it difficult to cope; Ernst's letters were brimful of love; he was deeply concerned that she shouldn't be carrying anything heavy. She should contact the doctor the moment she felt concerned. He hoped very much to be there for the birth. They telephoned one another several times, and in these days a telephone call was still very much an event.[15]

Her second child, Hartmut, was born on March 10, 1940, but Ernst was unable to get leave to be with her. However a few days later he did manage it, to their great relief and joy.[16] It was very late at night when he arrived. Lilo had already fallen asleep.

> *Then suddenly there was Ernst standing at the food of the bed. 'Lilo,' he enquired quietly. He had come in the back door, and already made himself comfortable and I hadn't noticed a thing. And then he knelt down beside my bed and said, 'Lilo, I am so happy!' It was the high point of our lives, full of happiness and deep thankfulness. Indeed it was the high point of our marriage.*[17]

Things began to go downhill after that, Lilo reflected much later.

For all her anxieties, though, she knew that in the village her task was to start building their family life together, to care for the new baby, to support Ernst as he helped to make Germany strong, and to welcome him back home again once the dust had settled as her husband, the father of her children, the popular schoolteacher in Wrohm. So she got on with her homemaking.

Then, after the eight-month break, the so-called phony war came to an end with the German invasion of Luxembourg, the Netherlands, Belgium, and France on May 10. Another quite extraordinary and speedy victory was the result. Hitler strode through Paris on June 23, and by June 25 the

14. Lilo to Ernst, December 31, 1939.
15. Ernst to Lilo, March 6, 1940.
16. Ernst, to Lilo, March 14, 1940.
17. Lilo to Eva Falkemeier, April 24, 1946; Eva was the wife of one of Ernst's comrades; he had stayed with them, and Eva was to become a lifelong friend of Lilo's after the war.

armistice was signed. Ernst experienced these almost incredible victories in the West in the officer training camp in Potsdam, near Berlin. He had moved there after his initial period in Lübeck. His letters to Lilo from Potsdam, from the end of May until August 1940 paint a vivid picture of the German army's training of its conscripted officers. At twenty-eight, Ernst was older than many of those taking the course, and was far more conscientious than most. The mix of practical and theoretical instruction kept him on the go, day and night. Film shows and sports, such as handball games, offered some relaxation.

It was midsummer and the weather was warm, their rooms at times stiflingly hot. He was highly impressed, though, with the accommodation: four men to a room; in his there was someone from Munich, from Berlin, from the Rhineland, and himself from Schleswig-Holstein. The field beds were of superior quality, with springs and mattresses; each boasted a bedside table, a washbasin with mirrors, and a shelf for toiletry; he appreciated the excellent showers, hot and cold. There were four large cupboards in the workroom, four writing desks, a cupboard for their boots, and a waste paper basket. The rooms were cleaned for them. He found the food somewhat uninspired, though: little in the way of vegetables or fruit; he mentions noodles, and potato soup without meat. Lilo, though, was quick to supplement this with parcels of goodies from Wrohm.

The daily timetable ran as follows:

6:30–11:00 a.m. training outdoors

11:30 a.m. lunch, followed by some time for a siesta, at least in theory

2:00–6:30 p.m. theoretical instruction

7:00 p.m. meal

Asked by Lilo if he was enjoying his time at the camp, he said he would infinitely prefer either being at Wrohm with his wife and children and at his teaching, or at the Front, so he could help to *den Feind schlagen* (defeat the enemy), but he found positive sides to the experience, too. He had learnt a lot, and had developed the leadership skills he had already gained in the *Landjahr* program and in his work with the Hitler Youth. The instructors were good on the whole. They could be pretty free with criticism and abuse, however, if one messed up.[18]

---

18. Ernst to Lilo, July 4, 1940.

Most of his young comrades capitalized on any free time to swarm into Berlin and tried their luck with the women there; he saw his time in Potsdam much more conscientiously as a patriotic duty. He did enjoy the manly activities; it appealed to the teenager in him, *einer jugendhaften Ecke in meiner Seele* (a youthful "nook" in my soul); as a young guy he had been stirred by Karl May's sagas set in the Wild West.[19] He was reminded of them at times, not least during the cross-country horse riding. His heart was always back in Wrohm, though.[20] Virtually every letter of his talks about the children; he kissed them affectionately in his imagination; he was forever sending them presents and children's postcards.

There was too much of the usual military spit and polish for him at Potsdam. More useful were the various theoretical sessions and those on draftsmanship. In the evenings, apart from occasional sentry duties, he was kept busy studying material from the day's classes and preparing himself for the next day. He hardly had time to hear the radio news, and rather resented the lack of time for reflection. He was, as he wrote to Lilo, an idealist, someone who liked to distance himself from outward things. "It's a pity. I would like to go down into the depths of the soul and offer you lovingly the modest sacrifice of a great and strong manly love. But never mind, dearest, the war will soon be over."[21] One is struck by his rather overblown language, and by his strong sense of duty.

The summer of 1940 was, of course, a time of supreme confidence in Germany. France had been conquered, and Ernst predicted that England would feel the full force of the Luftwaffe by early July. The Britons wouldn't know what had hit them.[22] The letters constantly remind us, though, that these two young people are first and foremost lovers. Ernst's greatest delight came from reading her letters, the longer the better, and he was frustrated that he found so little time to write back to her.[23] Neither of them tired of reiterating the depth and exclusivity of their love for each other. "I cannot go to sleep without thinking of you. Any moment of freedom from study leads my thoughts to you, beloved Lilo," he wrote from Potsdam. "No man

19. Ernst to Lilo, June 22, 1940; novels by Karl May (1842–1912), set in the Wild West and featuring the characters of Winnetou and Old Shatterhand, were very popular with young German boys.

20. Ernst to Lilo, August 4, 1940.

21. Ernst to Lilo, June 12, 1940.

22. Ernst to Lilo, June 18, 1940; June 22, 1940: . . . *das den Briten Hören und Sehen vergeht.*

23. Ernst to Lilo, May 21, 1940; May 26, 1940.

could love a woman more warmly and inwardly than I do." One superlative follows another as they tried to do justice to their feelings.[24]

"I am unspeakably happy," he wrote: "I so long for you." The letter he had just received from her had triggered off a wave of joy. "My beloved, you know how passionately I love you. I could not go on without your letters, without knowing with utter certainty that this woman loves me in life and death, for better or worse." When he is away from Lilo, he takes her heart along with him, and can feel it beating. "I am full of yearning and need love so much. . . . Deep love has to find fulfilment, oneness."[25]

They were passionately committed to each other, and for Ernst this meant strict monogamy. Though the sexual urge often threatened to overpower him, his deep longing for Lilo enabled him to resist it. He had nothing but contempt for those who sought *billige Entladung* (cheap release) from casual sex. He was glad that he found others in the Potsdam training academy who felt as he did, and they talked openly about their sexuality, agreeing on the need for self-control and absolute loyalty to one's wife.[26]

A few precious days leave allowed Lilo and Ernst to meet again, but it only sharpened his longing to be with her. "My one and only lass, I so fiercely long for your love. . . . I need you desperately right now. You know I cannot live without you. . . . I'm coming, darling, I'm coming very soon."[27] As soon as he was back in Potsdam, he longed either to return home or get to the Front. He hated missing her birthday in August. He'd had enough of the training exercises, and the elaborate farewell ceremonies annoyed him with their wastefulness and drunken carousing.[28] His last letter from Potsdam on August 8 looked forward to returning home to Wrohm.

By August 19, though, he was back in the training camp at Lübeck, very much out of sorts, as it appeared he had to start training new recruits, mainly students and those just out of school, and it was back to life in barracks. As a newly fledged officer, Ernst also had to acquire a ceremonial sword, which did not particularly impress him either, especially as it hit the pocket hard.[29] In early November, though, he managed a weekend visit to

24. Ernst to Lilo, June 9, 1940.
25. Ernst to Lilo, May 9, 1940; February 3, 1940; February 13, 1941.
26. Ernst to Lilo, June 12, 1940; he uttered similar contempt for the sexual vagaries of the men in the Lübeck camp: Ernst to Lilo, October 17, 1940.
27. Ernst to Lilo, July 31, 1940.
28. Ernst to Lilo, July 22, 1940; July 31, 1940; August 2, 1940; August 7, 1940.
29. Ernst to Lilo, August 19, 1940; September 4, 1940.

Lilo in Spantekow, where she was visiting her family; and he enjoyed the chance to play with the children.³⁰

By December 1940 Ernst found himself in France, posted to Pornic, a little fishing village in the Bretagne, as part of a coastal defense unit. It was all very comfortable and uneventful, although he found it strange to be living in enemy territory. The inhabitants went about their business as if nothing had happened, or that was his perception at least. They talked to him quite naturally when he was out and about or shopping.³¹ He practiced his French every day and read Alexander Dumas.

He would walk along the coast and waxed lyrical about sun and sea. The fields, with their shrub-covered boundary lines, reminded him of his home landscape in Schleswig-Holstein. Every town had its National Socialist welfare center for the troops, with free food, and German girls behind the counters. He describes how he and his fellows were overcome by a "marvelous sense of togetherness" when they listened to a speech by the Führer.³²

His thoughts were already turning to Christmas. He imagined himself with Lilo in Wrohm, listening to music together. He couldn't bring himself to ask for leave, though, as most of his comrades had spent their last Christmas on the Front, but he assured her of his fervent longing for her, and sent home packages of oranges, stockings, and other gifts. Every letter from her lifted his spirit, he wrote. He looked forward to leave in February, imagining the baby in his cot, and his sweet little toddler peering over the fence. Every day he was with Lilo, heart and soul. She was his anchor, the midpoint of his life, in her he found *Geborgenheit* (a deep inner security), and this love sang through his work and surged through his days.³³

Like his comrades he went on a shopping spree for goods unobtainable in Germany, but was disturbed by the *Haltlosigkeit* (lack of moral boundaries) of his companions, making particular reference to masturbation and brothel visits.³⁴ He realized how much of the special electricity of their own

30. Ernst to Lilo, November 14, 1940.
31. On the varied and changing interactions of French people and their German occupiers cf. Vinen, *The Unfree French*, 99–132.
32. Ernst to Lilo, December 11, 1940.
33. Ernst to Lilo, November 14, 1941.
34. Ernst to Lilo, January 12, 1941.

wedding night derived from their self-control over the years, both of them coming to it as virgins.[35]

He trusted that Lilo agreed with him that participating in the birth of a new Germany and a new world order made their separation and their personal sacrifices worthwhile.[36] On Christmas Day 1940 there were the traditional decorations in the rooms; the Christmas tree; mulled wine; plates of nuts, figs, chocolate, and biscuits. They sang the traditional carols, and reminisced about past Christmastides, and even the young lieutenant managed a few words. Then Ernst himself spoke for ten minutes about Christmas at the Front and read out a traditional story. The military chaplain held a service in the nearby Catholic church, which Ernst found brought tears to his eyes. Back in his own room, he thought of the family at Wrohm and opened his presents and read his letters.[37]

The routines of army life are described in lively detail in his letters home. They conducted regular patrols, went for forty-kilometer (!) marches; a five-hour ride through the wintry countryside really toughened one up. Ernst loved working with horses, and being fit was the precondition for feeling on top of things, the very elixir of life. It was hard, though, after a tiring day, to mount sentry duty for part of the night. His prize in a pistol-shooting completion had been a copy of the *Die Westfront (Western Front)*, a "wonderful" soldiers' magazine, which he promised to send on to Lilo.[38] He was sure the war would be over by the summer. The Führer would see to that.[39]

Ernst's promotion to lieutenant came through in January 1941, which improved their finances. At a reception for a theater group, he sat for the first time with his fellow officers and was pleased to see that there was nothing stiff or formal about the occasion.[40] Films were often available, though he was seldom enthusiastic about them. One based on Gottfried Keller's *Kleider Machen Leute (Clothes Maketh the Man)* was more enjoyable.

The news from Wrohm was not that good. Life in the village had always been Spartan, but the winter of 1940–1941 had been particularly

---

35. *Welch Maßen Seligkeit können zwei reine Herzen einander bereiten! Welch Spannung [?] lag in unserer Unberührtheit!* Ernst to Lilo, March 23, 1941.
36. Ernst to Lilo, December 14, 1940; December 15, 1940.
37. Ernst to Lilo, December 25, 1940.
38. Ernst to Lilo, December 25, 1940.
39. Ernst to Lilo, January 1, 1941.
40. Ernst to Lilo, January 10, 1941.

severe, with knee-deep snow, which cascaded from the roof. Lilo had to shovel the snow away every morning. It lay on top of a thick layer of ice in the yard. She had to lug endless buckets of water to the washtub for the weekly laundering, which had been not at all easy when she was pregnant with their second child. The clothes froze in the bucket where they had been soaked overnight, emerging stiff as a board; frequently the pipes froze. The toilet was just a bucket, which stank in the summer and froze in the winter; she then had to use boiling water to dispose of the contents. Sometimes the bucket was frozen to the ground and immovable. The house itself was bitterly cold in winter, especially the bedroom. The heating didn't work properly. "The icy east wind draws the last bit of warmth out of the rooms . . . ; one's hands freeze trying to clean them. The houses just don't thaw out any more." It was hard to get coke (coal residue) or peat for the stove. The water tank burst. All food, of course, was rationed.[41]

Writing from the milder Bretagne winter, Ernst was appalled at these conditions, the grim weather in Wrohm, and the heating problems.[42] The snow had one good side, though. Sledges and ice skates soon appeared, and Lilo hugely enjoyed the chance to indulge again in sledging and ice-skating.[43]

As a lieutenant now, Ernst had to lead his platoon in his first major field exercise at the end of January 1941, and he prepared for it meticulously, knowing that he had to be ready to make the right decisions at the right times in order to offer effective leadership.[44] The training ground was icy, and turned into a sea of mud as the thaw set in. He described getting up at five in the morning, riding out for two hours in pouring rain, then practicing sharpshooting. Throughout the day he was busy, supervising various activities, and ending up by overseeing the cleaning of the rifles at seven o'clock in the evening. It was nonstop! In February his company's stay in the Bretagne came to an end. There was a festive meal and the usual toasts and speeches.[45]

Lilo meanwhile was getting through the winter in Wrohm. Money was tight, and she sent Ernst meticulous accounts of what she had spent. Every penny was watched. Food, heating, children's clothes and shoes, dental

41. Lilo to Ernst, January 23, 1940; January 30, 1941.
42. Ernst to Lilo, February 5, 1941.
43. Lilo to Ernst, January 11, 1941.
44. Ernst to Lilo, January 14, 1941.
45. Ernst to Lilo, January 19, 1941; February 5, 1941.

bills, the church tax—all swallowed up money, as countless letters testify. There was no phone in the house. On one occasion she had to rush to her neighbors' house in her nightie, a coat flung over it, her stockings trailing, to catch a phone call from Ernst.[46]

Visits to the dentist or to Ernst's mother in neighboring villages were negotiated by bike. She had endless problems with her poor teeth, and this was to continue throughout the war, involving painful root extractions. Train travel, third class, took her on the occasional longer trip to Hamburg or even to far-off Pomerania, to her family in Spantekow and Swinemünde. Changing trains with a small child and her luggage could be something of a nightmare.

Lilo was responsible during her husband's absence for the large schoolhouse garden; as spring began to warm the soil, she saw to the planting, weeding, and harvesting of the potatoes, onions, carrots, beans, peas, asparagus, and spinach; in the autumn she preserved large quantities of plums, peaches, cherries, and strawberries; she made compote and jam; with the big crop of apples she made jelly, and she dried apples for the winter, which was no picnic in the wet summer of 1940. Shortages of sugar, too, could be a problem. Some apples were given away to friends, or sold. Lilo was helped with these various challenges by her father, her old school friend Ruth Krügler, and some neighbors, but initially sympathy was limited, as only one other village family had a man away in the army. The planting, weeding, and harvesting ate up Lilo's time, and at times it got her down. There was simply far too much to do.[47]

In the warmer months, though, the vegetable garden was a godsend. On the whole, house and garden were like a whiff of heaven for her:

> *It's Saturday evening. So peaceful outside, wonderful air, the last rays of the sun reach the dining room, a few bees drone away in the cherry blossoms. I've just been walking through the garden, just as you used to love doing. What I would give to wander through it with you and inspect the vegetable beds, the shrubs, the trees. I'm really enjoying working in the garden much more now. How wonderful it will be when we look after it together. The first flowers are out on the strawberry plants, the cherry blossom is a bit meager this year, but the little plum tree at the front with the big apricot plums is blooming, the early potatoes are shooting up and tomorrow we'll have the first asparagus shoots in the soup. I've been hoeing the carrots. The*

---

46. Lilo to Ernst, March 26, 1940.
47. Lilo to Ernst, April 28, 1941.

> *meadow beyond the garden is a carpet of yellow flowers. How happy we could be! My heart is heavy when I think of you, but during the day the sparkling eyes of the children chase away these thoughts.*[48]

Lilo was very open about her own health: her sleeplessness and discomfort during pregnancy, especially when Ernst was absent before the birth of her son in March 1940; after the birth her breasts were hard as stone and sore, and constipation plagued her. She was ecstatic, however, about her little boy. Her own mother had shown her very little love, and she was determined to pour out love on her children. Although nothing could replace Ernst, she needed something to love, and the children benefited. Lilo appears to have been a very caring mother. They snuggled into bed with her first thing in the morning. She was inordinately proud of both children, as she confessed in countless letters to Ernst, and not only gave them affection and security, but observed their behavior and language closely and found ways to stimulate them.

"I wish you could experience our little girl," she wrote, "for this lovely time won't come again." Heinke was beginning to talk a little already, was more and more active, so sweet, the "wee mouse"; it was fascinating to see her becoming more mobile, propping herself up on the sides of the cot or the wall, drinking from the bottle on her own, so lively and full of life, dashing everywhere, arms stretched out in front of her to keep her balance; sticking everything into her mouth; rushing out of the house onto the street; playing with her bricks and her balls; and kissing her Dad's photo and saying "Papa."

> *No doubt about it, the wee lass is my sunshine. You've no idea what a gem she is. She runs around on her own more and more as one day succeeds another, hands me all her wooden building blocks, which I have to take back from her. When little brother gets the bottle of milk she thinks it's for her and can't believe that it's not. She has a great appetite, with a special love for tart, gobbles up a huge piece of it.*

At times, of course, she could be difficult, yelling in protest when she had to come out of the bath; her brother, Hartmut, was more contented and better behaved, a great eater, and "so sweet." His smile was like a ripe, red apple.[49] His sister was very good with him. Hartmut yahooed for joy when he found he could walk on his own. He was hyperactive, with an enormous appetite

---

48. Lilo to Ernst, May 24, 1941; she gives a detailed description not only of the vegetable garden but of the glorious flowers a month later; June 19, 1941.

49. Lilo to Ernst, February 29, 1940; March 26, 1940.

for food and for life.⁵⁰ He stuffed tomatoes into his mouth as if they were apples.

Letter after letter offered vivid accounts of the children, their clothes, their language, and their antics:

> *Ach, if only you could have seen your sweet little boy. A real young lad in his checked shirt, red pants with shoulder straps and red knee socks. And our wee kitten (Muschi) who is already embarking on her own childhood way and reports to me her experiences at the top of her voice. This evening she headed off with 'Auntie' Johannsen to milk the cows. What fun that was! She talks* platt *(lower German) with Frau Johannsen, understanding everything the latter says.*⁵¹ *What joy it gives her, collecting the eggs, giving water to the bull! She sings a song and as a reward gets an egg. And then this morning she was at kindergarten. Oh, with what aplomb she set off. She joined in the play happily, and loved the swings. I am expecting a lot from the kindergarten. It's so nice there, learning to wash their hands, sit on the potty, have breakfast etc. Yes, Pappy, we already have a grown up daughter, you know? She's miles ahead of the other children. What a wealth children bring; each day produces countless joys.*

When Lilo saw the kids naked in the bath, she felt like gobbling them up in sheer delight! The two-year-old Heinke was unusually aware of others. She noticed when her mother was upset, and tried to comfort her.⁵²

Lilo saw Ernst's energy and intelligence reflected in Hartmut, in the little toddler's gestures. Hartmut was never still, always rushing around, *ein unbeschreiblicher Quirl* (an incredible live wire), sticking his finger into the entrance of the beehive, and paying for it with countless stings.⁵³ He chased the ducks, hens, and geese around the yard, and was beginning to enjoy picture books, saying *wauwau* when he saw a dog. He loved knocking down the wooden building bricks. He could be quite a handful at times.⁵⁴ Heinke at two and a half was fascinated by fairy tales such as "Little Red Riding

50. Lilo to Ernst, April 13, 1941.
51. Lilo reports on Heinke: *Plattdeutsch kommt sie auch schon an. 'Mama, luren'; und 'hört Heinke tau'; 'und na' Hus gon.' Wenn ich aber mit ihr platt schnacke, ist es ihr doch recht komisch.* ("She is already talking in the local dialect. 'Look, Mama'; 'Listen to Heinke'; 'and go home.' But she looks askance if I talk to her in dialect.) Lilo to Ernst, June 20, 1941.
52. Lilo to Ernst, May 29, 1941.
53. Lilo to Ernst, September 2, 1941.
54. Lilo to Ernst, October 24, 1941.

The False Sense of Peace

Hood" and by the poem "The Giant Timpetu." She couldn't hear the stories often enough.[55] Ernst's colleague, Frau Butenschön, gave the two children, "my dear Sommer children," a charmingly illustrated collection of lullabies, *Guten Abend, Gut' Nacht! (Good Evening, Good Night!)*.[56]

The books Lilo and Ernst bought for their own children included the Nazi propaganda picture book *Soldatenspiel (Playing at Soldiers)*, illustrated by Curt Junghändel. Its brightly colored illustrations show helmeted five-to-seven-year-old children, both girls and boys, flourishing rifles, swords, and grenades, manning a field gun, building bridges, and attending field hospitals; but most of the children's books were gentle and child-centered, like Erwin Jäkel's *Für dich und mich! (For You and for Me!)*, though it did exude a rather moralistic tone. The same was true of Ernst Füge's *Hullebulletöpflein*. This tells the story of a poor woman who is gifted a magic pot but in the end is doomed to ruin by her exorbitant greed. Hans Probst's pop-up book portrays *Die Weihnachtsengelein (The Little Christmas Angels)*; and in Hagdis Hollriede's *Weiß dir und mir (Lovely House)*, seven little girls peep out of their house clutching dolls, flowers, and kittens and dream of their (predictable) future roles as mothers or nurses.[57] Other books possessed by the young marrieds were Theodor Storm's best-selling fairy tale *Der kleine Häwelmann (The Little Havelmann)*. Then there was the charming fantasy, *Der Zuckertütenbaum (The Sugar Cone Tree)*: after Christmas Ruprecht, Saint Nicholas's offsider, comes to the land of the dwarfs with his magic onion and plants the new sugar cone tree. A dreamy, romantic note is struck by Lely Kempin's *Die Heilige Insel (Sacred Island)*, which has a pre-Raphaelite young girl wandering naked through an enchanted island; we see her sitting on a rock, her long hair flowing in the wind. Like countless other families they had a (cheap) edition of Wilhelm Busch's *Max und Moritz*, two rascals engaging in roguish and marvelously illustrated adventures.[58] Elsa Butenschön gave the children an attractive little book, which took the reader through each month of the year, *Heinzel wandert durch das Jahr (Heinzel wanders through the Year)*.[59] Wartime, then, did not

---

55. Lilo to Ernst, September 18, 1941.

56. Busch-Schummann, ed., *Guten Abend, Gut' Nacht!*

57. Junghändel, *Soldatenspiel*; Jäkel, *Für dich und mich!*; Füge, *Das Hullebulletöpflein*; Heinrich and Sextus, *Der Zuckertütenbaum ein Bilderbuch*; Kempin, *Die Heilige Insel*; Probst, *Die Weihnachtsengelein*.

58. Hollriede, *Weiß dir und mir*; Busch, *Max und Moritz*.

59. Bohatta-Morpurga, *Heinzel Wandert durch das Jahr*.

mean a diet of war books. The children were introduced to a wide range of imaginative literature.

Her loneliness began to take its toll on Lilo, though, and when her maid, Herta, handed in her notice in the spring of 1941, it really rattled her. Evidently others in the village had put Herta up to it. It coincided with the fear that Ernst would not get leave at Whitsun. She wept buckets, and wrote bitterly: "Oh, well, let's get on with it. I'm used to misery and in Wrohm can savor all the 'advantages' available to a single woman. What a nice prospect! The house, the garden, cooking, washing, preserving." On top of that she had to keep a vigilant eye on two lively little children and cope with the raids of the "Tommies" at night. The British bombers on their path to Hamburg sometimes dropped a bomb or two on Wrohm. She got no sympathy, though, from Ernst's mother in Tellingstedt. Just a shrug of the shoulder![60] Village life was no bed of roses. It never had been. But it was about to get much worse.

---

60. Lilo to Ernst, May 17, 1941.

3

Why Hitler? Why National Socialism?

> *We had fed the heart on fantasies,*
> *The heart's grown brutal from the fare;*
> *More substance in our enmities*
> *Than in our love.*
>
> —W. B. YEATS, 1928

As THE FOCUS OF the war shifted from the West to the East again, and before we turn to the confrontation with Russia (in what was to be known as Operation Barbarossa), it seems timely to ask what these vast geopolitical events meant to our young couple. How did it affect their joint enthusiasm for the National Socialist cause? How did they see their own little world, their love for each other, their delight in their children, and their hopes for the future in the context of this titanic military and political struggle? National Socialism not only glorified war. It was a death cult, as its ceremonies, its songs, and its literature make abundantly clear. Why did Ernst and Lilo not see this?

Ernst had been a conscientious, successful, and much loved village schoolteacher in Schleswig-Holstein, way up in the north. In his letters he comes across as a thoughtful and caring father and partner; he does his best to mediate in the tensions within the family, much of it stemming from his mother's criticisms of his young bride; and he upholds high standards of personal morality.[1]

There is no doubt, however, of his dedication to the National Socialist cause. He had been swept away by the atmosphere of the Nuremberg Rally in September 1935: "An electric charge ran through the ranks, as we marched past Adolf Hitler with our flags raised high." They had been on the go since 3:30 a.m. (!), and he was one of the flag-bearers.[2] When Hitler ordered the occupation of the Rhineland in 1936, Ernst dismissed the anxiety in Schalkholz about an imminent war as the clacking of a few women. "We rejoiced at Hitler's momentous action; Germany is now free. The petty minded just want their comfortable life. But we need to see the larger picture."[3] "Without Adolf Hitler it would never have been possible. I believe in his mission, not only for Germany, but for Europe too, for the world." Germany's policies would turn the world upside down. "What a Führer, what a nation!"[4]

True, he had no great enthusiasm for war, the memory of the Great War being too close, "but the old world is breaking down. England, France, Poland will soon be dealt with."[5] He had been sanguine up to the very last moment that war could be avoided. Only a few *gewissenslose Elemente* (immoral types) in Britain were gung ho for a fight.[6] "The main thing is for us to stand in solidarity with our Führer." Faced with Germany's determination, the others would see the light and give way.[7]

His language, the talk of "iron will" and resistance to the red hordes, at times reflected Party ideology. As he wrote to Lilo, "At the end of the day, let's recall that we both are German and are constantly aware of the *Aufgabe* (task) that lies ahead."[8] "I know that our people has arisen to put its *Reich*

---

1. There is an edginess to Lilo's relationships, not only with Ernst's mother, but with other members of the family and in-laws, such as the Knolls in Berlin; many letters speak of Lilo in great distress, and of Ernst being very upset, and urging moderation on everyone; Lilo should abandon all these gloomy thoughts and not disturb him with *häßlichen* (nasty) letters; Ernst to Lilo, February 19, 1940.
2. Ernst to Leni and Karl, September 20, 1935.
3. Ernst to Lilo, March 7, 1936.
4. Ernst to Leni, March 12, 1936.
5. Ernst to Lilo, September 4, 1939.
6. Ernst to Lilo, September 27, 1939.
7. Ernst to Lilo, October 23, 1939.
8. Ernst to Lilo, October 4, 1939.

on a firm footing once for all; and to defend it."⁹ He embraced National Socialist educational ideals but also its foreign policy aims, a Europewide economy with Germany at its head. He even considered the option of resettling in the east after the war, in line with Hitler's *Lebensraum* policies.¹⁰

He hailed the invasion of Yugoslavia and Greece in April 1941 as a decisive intervention that would bring peace closer. Hitler's military leadership was genial. Its purpose was the reordering of the world and the recognition at long last of Germany's proper place in it. The war was "providing the German people with a firm foundation for its existence for hundreds of years to come. It certainly is repellent to watch and it devastates the nations. It would be so much better for it to be over. Yes, war is evil."¹¹

Although on occasion he felt depressed, and although he did not always get on with his fellow officers, Ernst's temperament was a sanguine one, confident of decisive changes ahead and of imminent victory.¹² Like so many Germans when the Russian campaign began, he felt it would be over in a matter of months. The buoyancy of Ernst's early reports from Russia seems in retrospect incredible, but of course reflected the flow of information available to him and a widespread national mood. He was also convinced that by the summer of 1941 the English would be finished.¹³ Even in December 1941 he wrote from the Russian Front of his confidence in the *Endsieg* (final victory). By this time he was very much involved in a grim, unremitting struggle and was increasingly aware of the depth of Russian resilience and resistance. "It's not always easy to endure, but we are upheld as we think of the momentous nature of our task."¹⁴

If we inquire about his primary motivation it appears to have been patriotism, together with a strong sense of *Pflicht* (duty), a word that was often in his mouth. Family, *Volk*, and God were for him inseparable. "We know that we stand here for the sake of Germany. 'Enthusiasm for war,' I hear someone say. Anything but! All of us here would much rather be with wife and child, at our chosen vocation or productive work, but within us

9. Ernst to Lilo, January 11, 1940.

10. Ernst to Lilo, February 5, 1941.

11. Ernst to Lilo, June 5, 1941; *[Der Krieg] gibt dem deutschen Volk heute seine Existenzgrundlage für Jahrhunderte. Seine Erscheinungsform ist allerdings abscheulich und schrecklich sucht er die Völker heim. Besser ist es, ihn hinter sich zu haben. Nun, der Krieg ist übel;* Ernst to Lilo, November 11, 1941.

12. Ernst to Lilo, May 28, 1941; June 17, 1941.

13. Ernst to Lilo, May 16, 1941.

14. Ernst to Lilo, December 8, 1941.

glows this iron resolve: our nation, our dear ones, should not have to endure the sort of wretched misery we see before us. We have to stand here to protect you from this red horde."[15] "The aim of the war is so grandiose that it continually fills me with enthusiasm. What are our little concerns compared with that? The Führer is building our *Reich* and we are able to help him. Is that not a cause to rejoice?"[16] Together with his patriotism, then, is the exhilaration of being involved in world-shaking events, of contributing to a fundamental reshaping of the map of Europe.

> *The war is our war, and it is a life-and-death affair. All the difficulties are as nothing compared with what would ensue if the Reds or the British were victorious. We would never be happy again. Every day we can see with our own eyes the wretchedness of the people, the poverty and distress under Stalin's régime. All those involved in this campaign have had their eyes opened. They know that compromise is out of the question. We either win everything or lose everything. Gradually a holy rage engulfs us. One's heart wants to return home and the yearning for that is massive and yet the Reich, our great concept, stakes its claim on us. The Bolshevik is still at it, even if in the last agonies. The Bolshevik defies our Reich and our heart's longing. Hence the rage!*[17]

There are no *Heil Hitler*s and little explicit National Socialist jargon in Ernst's letters to Lilo, or indeed in those of his close comrades. There is scant evidence of anti-Semitism in the letters, either, but it is clear that he had swallowed the propaganda that the Jews were responsible for the Russian scorched-earth policy in their retreat from Dünaburg. He was glad that the *Schutzstaffel* (SS) had "restored order" there. He was aware, of course, of the need to prove his own Aryan ancestry; he mentions the notorious film *Jud Süss* with approval. As a teacher he must also have used the racist materials provided by the National Socialist Teachers' Union.[18] Seeing a prisoner of war camp in France housing many black Africans, he commented, "Dreadful to think of having to fight against people like that."[19]

---

15. Ernst to Lilo, December 3, 1941.
16. Ernst to Lilo, September 28, 1941.
17. Ernst to Lilo, November 10, 1941.
18. Ernst to Lilo, July 3, 1941; few other films are explicitly mentioned in the correspondence; Lilo also mentions *Jud Süss*, Lilo to Ernst, October 24, 1940; and enjoyed the documentary film warning about spies: *Feind hört mit*; Lilo to Ernst, November 17, 1940.
19. Ernst to Lilo, May 1, 1941.

Why Hitler? Why National Socialism?

As for Lilo, she too read the *Völkischer Beobachter*, listened each night at 8:00 p.m. to the news on the radio (now that they had managed to buy one), and listened to Goebbels's exegesis of events. What she knew of politics and of the wider world came through the National Socialist media. Only those, of course, with international contacts had any independent access to the news. She would have been like hundreds of thousands of other young mothers, relying on her husband for guidance on the broader social and political issues. She was elated, as we have seen, by the Third Reich's early successes: the bombing of Norway, the blitzkrieg in France—and she was hopeful that the defeat of England would soon follow.

However, she was not primarily a political being. The lens through which she saw the world was that of family: husband, children, and homemaking. The rhetoric of heroic sacrifice for the Fatherland left her cold, and she measured the lofty proclamations about *Volksgemeinschaft* (folk solidarity) against the patent self-interest of most of her farming neighbors, though some, like the Doose family in Wrohm, were hospitable and extraordinarily helpful, asking her round on New Year's Day, bringing little gifts of milk and carrots. "I know these farmers. Nothing there but egoism and materialism." She was aware of countless black market deals going on. "Authentic peasant life, all that is empty prattle. Only 5 percent of all soldiers are brave and courageous, the rest are cowards, and only go along with it, because they must."[20] She noted cynically that many babies in the doctor's clinic were decked out in fancy clothing, which could only have come from Belgium.[21]

Her priority was holding her young family together. The war jeopardized this. "Our generation knows nothing but struggle, first at home, and then abroad."[22] She continued to hope against hope that Ernst could resume his teaching role and be released from the Front; it seems he was being considered for the *Aufbau* (intensive) school in Burg, and she begged him not to turn it down if the opportunity turned up; she kept asking him about this.[23] It involved training specially gifted children from the seventh school year on. Yet she did try to understand and share his enthusiasm for setting off for France as 1940 came to an end, just as he sought to empathize with her weariness with the war.

20. Lilo to Ernst, April 28, 1941.
21. Lilo to Ernst, December 11, 1940.
22. Lilo to Ernst, December 22, 1941.
23. Lilo to Ernst, February 16, 1940; January 5, 1941; March 14, 1941.

There is no hint at all in Lilo's reflections of explicit criticism of National Socialist policies, still less of Hitler; quite the contrary, she was vexed when she missed any of his speeches. "Yesterday the Führer addressed the *Winterhilfswerk* (Winter Relief Organization), mobilizing support for the needy. The love and enthusiasm for this man is limitless. Even over the radio it grips one's heart. . . . He found wonderful words for our German soldiers, above all for the German infantry."[24] She was full of praise for his splendid initiative in offering England a separate peace after the fall of France. His address on the radio in January 1941 convinced her (for the moment at least) that Germany would be victorious within the year.[25]

When she heard of Norwegians spitting at some of the German pilots who had parachuted to safety, she found such hatred incomprehensible.[26] Her world, in a nutshell, was a narrowly German one. There was little or no understanding for the English or the French, still less for the Poles or the Russians. As we have seen, she welcomed the campaign against France and the imminent invasion of England. She asked her husband about the destruction in French towns and villages, and wondered if every young Frenchman was either in captivity or dead. Was it true, she asked, obviously having heard another wild rumor, that the French women stand at their doors stark naked?[27]

These naïve comments were those of a young mother with little access to independent information. Lilo was impatient for the invasion of England to begin but, anticipating that it would entail considerable casualties, hoped it would be all over before Ernst had completed his training as an officer. Like Ernst's assistant teacher, Ella Butenschön,[28] she expected the English campaign to be as swift as that in France, and couldn't understand why the invasion had been so long delayed.[29]

---

24. Lilo to Ernst, February 25, 1940; features of the *Winterhilfswerk* (Winter Relief Organization) were highly imaginative posters, badges, and the use of enthusiastic young people for the house-to-house collection of donations; it was portrayed as a voluntary measure to combat hunger and cold; much of the huge amount of money raised, however, came from compulsory deductions from wages; cf. Bertolt Brecht's devastating critique of it in *Furcht und Elend des Dritten Reiches (Fear and Misery of the Third Reich)*, 113–15.

25. Lilo to Ernst, July 20, 1940; January 30, 1941.

26. Lilo to Ernst, March 21, 1940.

27. Lilo to Ernst, December 30, 1940; January 5, 1941.

28. Lilo to Ernst, June 30, 1940.

29. Lilo to Ernst, September 11, 1940.

Why Hitler? Why National Socialism?

She was obsessed by England because of the British bombers overhead, but National Socialist propaganda was also focusing heavily at this time on Britain's "criminal responsibility" for the war.[30] She even managed to convince herself that the massing of troops in East Prussia in the spring and summer of 1941 was in preparation for an invasion of England![31]

Even at a very early stage in 1940, however, the casualty lists unnerved her and led her to talk about this "terrible war." "The war can't be over quickly enough for me." It coarsened life. War (indeed the whole life of a soldier) hardened one, made one less sensitive—no doubt of necessity. How important, therefore, for Ernst to have comrades he could talk to on a personal, human level.[32]

As we have seen, Ernst was confident after the successful French campaign that Britain would be accounted for by July 1941, and that the troops could then return home. He really believed this, though it was also part of his ongoing campaign to reassure Lilo that he, his brother, Hans, and her brother, Dieter, would all be returning home soon: "There's no reason to be afraid. Tough cookies always survive."[33] In fact, all three of them were to perish within a couple of years.

Lilo was unconvinced by the reassurances. Her anxiety for her husband, for her brother, Dieter, and for her cousins, Hans-Joachim and Martin Friedrich, mingled with protectiveness towards her own children. Her alarm when stray bombs hit her village, which was on the flight path to Hamburg, also led her to be more realistic about the war than her husband.

From May 1940 on her letters betray how badly shaken she was by the British bombers droning overhead, and by the sound of flak and machine-gun fire. "The Tommies are with us every night," she wrote in June; her whole body had been shaking, and by the morning she was a total wreck. It was impossible to go down into the stinking cellar with the kids. "Dear, dear Ernst, when will this mad war come to an end?" she wrote. Leaflets had allegedly been dropped by the Royal Air Force, threatening gas attacks; "then we'd really be lost. How can they bomb us with such impunity?"[34] In

30. Cf. Evans, *The Third Reich at War*, 469.
31. Lilo to Ernst, June 4, 1941.
32. Lilo to Ernst, May 31, 1940; May 27, 1941.
33. Ernst to Lilo, June 9, 1940. *Furcht ist unbegründet, richtige Lausejungen hauen sich überall durch.*
34. Some of the leaflets showed some imagination: one bore the message: "People of Schleswig-Holstein, you can go on sleeping; it's the fat cats in Berlin we're heading for!" Lilo to Ernst, December 30, 1940.

her nightmares she saw bombs falling and herself and Ernst dying in one another's arms.[35]

By the end of 1940 she suspected that the war would drag on a long time. We can only guess what she and Ernst discussed on his leave in February after he left France. He only refers to it as having been a wonderful time.[36] Dependent as we are on the witness of their letters, it is ironic that we know least about their most precious times: when he was on leave and they were together at last.

The language of the Third Reich was that of *Blut und Boden* (blood and soil). Germany's well-being was the highest good imaginable. The key to history was the preservation of a pure racial stock and a return to the elemental realities of the natural world. For its adherents this new Reich utterly transcended all normal political, economic, and material considerations. The name of Germany was to be hallowed, and for its thousand-year destiny no sacrifice could be great enough. One's time, talents, and life were to be devoted to this sacred cause. The glorious future of the Reich gave meaning to everything. Its unfolding was like a dream coming true. Individuals perished, but the beloved Fatherland would remain.

The songbooks of the time offer a window into this world. The Hitler Youth songbook, for example, was one of those that Ernst possessed.[37] It drew, albeit selectively, on venerable regional traditions from all over Germany, from Frisia to Silesia; there were folk songs celebrating nature, romantic love, and hunting the deer; there were songs of weavers and miners, and ballads of the mercenaries (*Landsknechte*). It wasn't without simple canons, sea-shanties, and humorous material, either, and it even paid occasional homage to Schiller and Beethoven, or to Christian tradition. It included Matthias Claudius's beautiful children's song "*Der Mond ist aufgegangen*" ("The Moon Has Climbed into the Heavens"). The melodies were simple, rhythmical and catchy, designed for young folk marching through city streets or the countryside, or gathering around the campfire.

Patriotic songs set the tone, such as Ernst Moritz Arndt's 1812 "*Der Gott der Eisen wachsen ließ*" ("The God Who Created Iron"), which glorified those who took up sword and spear in the battle for the Fatherland: "Victory or the glorious death of the free!" The bulk of the contemporary Hitler Youth material from the 1930s echoes this sentiment. "God is the

---

35. Lilo to Ernst, January 5, 1940; June 27, 1940.
36. Ernst to Lilo, March 11, 1941.
37. Reichsjugendführung, ed., *Unser Liederbuch*. It contains some 250 songs.

fight, and the fight is our blood." "No more glorious death in the world" (than in battle). Its lyrics celebrate a divinely sanctioned revolution, a readiness for the ultimate sacrifice: *lewer dod als slav* ("better dead than slave").

To today's readers this may sound like the language of a death cult, but the young folk who sang these songs—to the beat of the drum, under flaring torches and the blood-red swastika flag—felt they were on the move to a better future. They were affirming their loyalty to the memory of their ancestors, committing their lives to the Führer, Adolf Hitler, and readying themselves to combat traitors, Jews, and Bolsheviks. With their comrades they would fight the good fight for freedom, work, and dignity. Their lives had meaning. They could make a difference.

The idealism of both Lilo and Ernst had been fired by this apocalyptic vision of a Reich pulsing with new life. Personal affluence, comfort, security, and family life—all this was supposed to be secondary. In practice this meant diverting material and human resources to the military struggle, channeling morality into the fight for racial and genetic purity, and opening up *Lebensraum*, new lands in the east. Liberal and democratic processes had fostered nothing but division and a craven submission to the unjust peace at Versailles. All that lay in the past. Hitler's genial leadership epitomized the Germanic values of unquestioned authority and communal solidarity. Personally and nationally this pointed the way ahead.

Ernst was a member of the SA and on occasion found it mind-deadening. But the marching and the singing captivated him:

> *Our life is marching, going forwards, that's the main thing, towards the infinite, the nameless one that we call God, an unfulfillable yearning, and yet revealed in Jesus. Our highest earthly goal—the nation—is a step towards God. To be of service to it is God's will for us. Germany is everything, because we are humans, Germans. Germany is the goal because we are the children of God.*[38]

When he heard about German troops marching into the Rhineland, the normally coolheaded teacher was swept into an ecstasy of joy. "Germany is experiencing the wedding feast of its life." He didn't want war, aware of the warnings of the fallen from the First World War; he himself didn't want to die, but it would be "a holy task to fight and to die for Germany." He felt torn in two, often: between his love of teaching and family, and the call to arms; between the fiddle and the sword.[39]

38. Ernst to Lilo, January 26, 1936.
39. Ernst to Lilo, March 8, 1936.

Yet for Ernst Sommer, love and comradeship, the personal and the political, and home life and military life complemented each other. He used the same word, "electricity" for his thrill at the Nuremberg Rally in 1935 and for their intercourse as a married couple:

> Love and comradeship are life's pillars. In love two people enhance one another, become one, are bonded together, find strength. We know how tender and joyful love can be from so many intimate, quiet or passionate hours. Love is the eternal feminine principle. And comradeship is its polar opposite. A woman must accept hardship with her man, if he is a real man, and stand by him in firm comradeship, when life gets stormy. . . . In manly comradeship new forces are released. The man desires struggle and action; achievement out here [on the Front] is what counts. The manly dimension has to emerge. Man and woman, comradeship and love are the high points of our life.[40]

The eternally feminine is starkly contrasted here with his understanding of masculinity. Yet Lilo is not altogether excluded from this comradely world, and Ernst was clear that commitment to work or to the army must never come in the way of their love for each other.

Lilo does not deploy this sort of exalted language. Her passion for the new Germany coincided with her passionate love for Ernst and her commitment to her children. Yet tension grew within her as the war snatched Ernst away from her, and as the increasingly global nature of the war, especially after the Russian campaign was launched, began to threaten her personal goal, which was to create a full and happy life around husband and children, home and vocation. "What have we had of our life? What have you had of your dear little children?" she would ask. The raging of the war had destroyed all that.[41] In the evening she looked at his picture before going to bed and cried bitterly at the mockery of her hopes. This was no life, she protested, it was a mere vegetable existence.[42]

The constant disappointments as far as leave was concerned underlined the marginalization of her personal dream, and alerted her to very different priorities from Ernst's. The bombing of her insignificant little village by the Tommies was the first ominous sign that the war, despite the blitzkrieg in Poland and France, was going to be protracted and costly. In

---

40. Ernst to Lilo, January 19, 1941.
41. Lilo to Ernst, August 26, 1941.
42. Lilo to Ernst, September 13, 1941.

her relative political and military innocence she had hoped that England could be knocked over quickly. Without allowing herself to think critically about Goering's or Hitler's strategies, she found herself increasingly puzzled, like countless other Germans, that the invasion of England was being delayed.

She tried to make sense of her husband's role in the war, and that of other family members—Hans Sommer; Dieter Strück, her brother; and her relatives Martin and Hans-Joachim Friedrich. She listened to the radio most evenings and read the papers. But she supplemented what she heard from these official quarters with conversations with neighbors or friends, especially after she moved to Pomerania. There are frequent hints of worry and pessimism among those to whom she talked, or in the letters she received. She scanned the death notices in the newspapers and observed the growing number of young wives dressed in black. She was aware of the heavy fighting and casualties around Staraja Russa. Even in little Wrohm there had been four fatalities by August 1941.[43] Nearer home, Hans, Ernst's brother, had been wounded twice, though not seriously. Dieter has also been wounded.[44]

The *Sicherheitsdienst* (Security Service) was well aware of the currents of discontent, worry, and low morale within the population. Goebbels himself was stridently critical of earlier, overconfident propaganda statements, which had raised expectations that were impossible to fulfill.[45] So Lilo's disquiets were widely shared; they just happen to be particularly well documented as a result of her outspoken letters. Her personal networks to some extent neutralized the official Party line; she would not have been alone in this either. What she may not have grasped was that National Socialist sloganizing provided a cover for the most naked careerism, cynicism, power plays, and sadism. How could she? Her experience after two years in the Landjahr, however, had alerted her, as we have seen, to the wild excesses of the rhetoric and the inhumanity of some of its leaders. Soldiers returning from the Front were often appalled and disgusted by the gold diggers who profited from the war, by the swagger and easy rhetoric of the *Goldfasaunen* (top brass of the Party).

---

43. Lilo to Ernst, August 17, 1941; August 26, 1941.

44. Lilo to Ernst, August 21, 1941.

45. Cf. Noakes, ed., *The German Home Front*, 509–80, esp. 537–38; Boberach, *Meldungen aus dem Reich*.

The worst blow for Lilo was the launching of Operation Barbarossa, the offensive against Russia in July 1941. From then on the National Socialist coupling of blood and soil began to come apart for her. More soil might be being won but at the cost of far too much German blood. Because it menaced her own personal project, the building up a happy family life, the Russian campaign was immediately recognized as a threat: the war became apostrophized for her as ghastly, frightening, and terrible. As murder. This did not lead to any fundamental critique of National Socialist policies, but Lilo increasingly raised doubts about the reality of the much-trumpeted *Volksgemeinschaft* (folk solidarity). She even voiced disappointment at particular statements of the Führer.

She had been shaken by the firebombing of Hamburg, which had begun in the autumn of 1940, and by the mass evacuations that followed, and Lilo could see no sense in war if such mass suffering of innocent civilians were to be the outcome. She even voiced, in the privacy and intimacy of letters to Ernst, pacifist thoughts.

The most direct threat to her own hopes came with the bombing of Wrohm itself, and the precipitate flight to Pomerania, of which more later. From then on her priority was the personal survival of Ernst and safeguarding her little family. She was still stirred by the remarkable victories of the initial Russian campaign, and proud of them, but she shuddered at the human cost in German lives. Her prayers, her admonitions to Ernst now focused on the one aim that Ernst should return home safe and well. He should not go chasing glory or the Iron Cross, though when it was awarded she was again immensely proud of him.

Lilo was acutely aware that he now stood in a completely different world from hers, and had been through extraordinary experiences. They were beginning to speak a different language. She was conscious of Ernst's dedication to his men and to the cause, but there is no hint in her letters that the fight against Bolshevism excited her. We have to keep reminding ourselves that she was first and foremost a young mother, still in her twenties, wondering if she, her husband, and her children had any sort of life ahead of them. As she read the reports and listened to the *Sondermeldungen* (special proclamations) on the radio, she focused almost exclusively on Ernst's well-being and safety. Everything was personalized. The war itself was privatized.

This brought a degree of clear-sightedness. Lilo was vividly aware of the long, forced marches the men had to endure, the blazing summer heat, the privations in terms of sleep and food, and then the threat of the coming winter. She was full of admiration for Ernst's personal courage and the army's professionalism. Anxiety, however, *schreckliche Angst* (terrible fear), was now the cantus firmus of her letters. Only one thought dominated her: she must get her dear Ernst back. "You have no idea what *Seelenkraft* (mental strength) is demanded of a soldier's wife. It is indescribable. [I couldn't endure] if I didn't have such an infinite love for you, and such a yearning for your love."[46]

She kept signaling that she was close to breaking down. "My enthusiasm for the war is gone. All I see is suffering and misery without end." She wondered if anyone would emerge from this hell alive.[47] She rejected the view that war was a necessity of nature, or in any way was *segensreich* (full of blessing). Everywhere one looked the contrary was true: it caused suffering, distress, and unhappiness; it robbed children of their fathers, and wives of their husbands. "Countless thousands had nothing left but their bare existence, every night bombing raids take lives, and the best of our soldiers lose their lives."[48] Her sympathy did not extend to the victims on the Allied side, civilian or military, but her emergent critique of war subverted the thrust of Goebbels's propaganda. The National Socialist glorification of war, its apprehension of life as struggle, was foreign to her.

Reading these letters one has to remind oneself again and again that we are in the midst of the unravelling of the most bloody and terrible war in human history, and among the most difficult and incomprehensible things for us to grasp is that Lilo's and especially Ernst's participation was undergirded and strengthened by their Christian faith. We meet again and again a conflation of Christian beliefs with an unquestioning identification with the National Socialist cause. Ernst undoubtedly saw himself as a Christian, his deep personal faith being a treasured inheritance from his mother. He advised the young people he had taught in Wrohm to proceed with their confirmation, although there were strong pressures against this from the Party.[49] He found deep peace and consolation in prayer, and expressed his sorrow that this was not the case for Lilo. It would be interesting to know how he dealt with history lessons in which the National Socialist line was

---

46. Lilo to Ernst, August 24, 1941.
47. Lilo to Ernst, September 3, 1941; September 15, 1941.
48. Lilo to Ernst, September 18, 1941.
49. Ernst to Lilo, April 3, 1941.

that the Christian church, from its forced conversions of the Saxons on, had consistently been a malign influence on Germanic society.

On the other hand, neither Ernst nor Lilo attended church regularly, nor is any regular pattern of Bible reading evident.[50] Ernst knew his New Testament well enough to choose one of the Gospels as his favorite. Lilo went to church mainly to play the organ, and enjoyed many of the hymns. Like many Germans theirs was a rather individualist, DIY spirituality, a household faith; but their convictions were genuine enough, quite carefully thought out in the case of Ernst. As we have seen, on a personal level he maintained a high standard of morality and was a very caring husband and a loving parent.

He tried to set out his beliefs to Lilo at the very beginning of their relationship. He admitted he was a dreamer who sought to make sense of life in all its fullness:

> *The aim, then, is the truth, and the truth is God, that is the completion of all things, the unity of mind, soul and will. This is never achieved in this earthly existence. Of course none of us arrived at an exclusive possession of the truth, I think of Lessing's parable of the rings.*[51] *Decisive is the awareness that the goal will never be reached, but committing oneself to pursue it. Our dynamic energies of mind, soul and will are able to release us from living just for the moment, as so many people do. In our soul we are rooted in the 'beyond,' in the mythical, in the world of the unconscious. Unlike the animal world we humans have the gift of reason, which affirms the pursuit of the best life possible and the bond to one's race, to one's Volk. That power from God which we call the will is the motor of our life, our innermost nature, given us to overcome human weakness. Soul, mind and will are inseparable.*

He wrote all this in what was essentially a love letter to Lilo, because he wanted her to share his deepest longings, to be able to trust herself to him, be one with him, and share the same inner purity and struggle for truth. Their own love for one another was part of this much larger commitment to land and people, which one sees in Christianity and in National Socialism.[52]

---

50. He did reciprocate the greetings from P. Kr., probably the Confessing Church pastor in Spantikow, Pastor Krause; Ernst to Lilo, September 8, 1941.

51. One wonders whether he had read Lessing's *Nathan der Weise* (*Nathan the Wise*), in which Judaism and Islam as well as Christianity, different ways to the truth, are symbolized by the three rings.

52. Ernst to Lilo, October 31, 1935.

Why Hitler? Why National Socialism?

At Christmastime Ernst liked to reflect on the need for "a spark from above"; for we hunger to see things whole, to sense the transcendent power that enables one to live a *"herrisches* (manly) life." God is too great to be captured by our minds. "God demanded faith."[53] Shortly before Christmas 1937 he talked of the *Tannenbaum* (Christmas tree), as the creation of the *urdeutschen Volksseele* (primeval soul of the German people); it stood for innocence, clarity, and illumination; if one viewed it as a child did, with a simple heart, one would sense the "hand of the almighty Creator, who will not keep us in the dark. Not rationality, but emotion is central." (Ernst quotes Hitler himself.)[54] Ernst describes God as "deep eternity."[55] Such language suggests a Germanic rather than a biblically based faith. Yet it is not quite as simple as that.

Our children, Ernst wrote to Lilo in March 1940, should not just talk of a loving God, but "should sense him as a power in their lives, not a kind uncle who showers one with good things, but they should learn to pray for strength and not arrogantly rely on themselves. Christ is the most marvelous *Verkünder* (revealer) of this God. He has brought God close in us in a childlike way, so that we can trust him." Ernst doesn't want his children asking for God's mercy but recognizing God's greatness, infinity, eternal nature, and their own littleness. Prayer, for Ernst, was about gratitude and was a source of inner strength, not a matter of pleading for this or that. The source of knowledge, of faith, and of all our strength was listening to the voice within. God helped those who helped themselves.[56] Such humility invested one with "due pride and confidence towards others. You are to God and nation what you are in yourself." "It's not necessary to take the Bible literally," he urges Lilo. "Don't get into debates about nonessential matters. Faith in God and recognition of the greatness of Christ are the key things. Ascension etc. is secondary, and so is the controversy about Paul."[57]

One assumes that these comments are based on previous discussions with Lilo. It may well be a reference to "German Christian" thinking, which tended to heroize the Aryan Christ and to dismiss the theology of the "Rabbi Paul." Some one-third of all Protestants had joined the so-called German Christian movement in Germany, which effectively acted as an ecclesiastical

---

53. Ernst to Leni and Karl, December 21, 1936.
54. Ernst to Leni and Karl, December 19, 1937; the reference to Hitler is his.
55. Ernst to Lilo, March 15, 1940.
56. Ernst to Lilo, December 16, 1941.
57. Ernst to Lilo, March 15, 1940.

arm of National Socialism. It was particularly strong in Schleswig-Holstein, after Bishop Adalbert Paulsen took over in 1933. Paulsen saw in Hitler's Reich a missionary opportunity for the church. He affirmed the exclusion of Jews from civic offices and was openly anti-Semitic, in accord with his view that "society, as God created it, has no rankings, no classes, but is determined by race."[58]

There is no evidence, however, of Ernst being part of the German Christian movement, though his language is very like theirs. He certainly believed that we come to God through Germany and then from God to Jesus. He saw no incompatibility in any of this. His soul, his nation, and his God were inseparable. He and Lilo were committed to "our God, our nation and our future family."[59]

It is likely that he was directly influenced by Rosenberg's *Der Mythus des 20. Jahrhunderts (Myth of the Twentieth Century).* His own copy of this book, carefully annotated and underlined, has survived. It is a very influential racist reading of German history, fiercely anti-Jesuit, tracing a new apostolic succession of Germanic faith through "Odin, Siegfried, Widukind, Friedrich II [Hohenstaufen], Eckhart [the mystic], von der Vogelweide, Luther, Friedrich I [of Prussia], Bach, Goethe, Beethoven, Schopenhauer, Bismarck"![60] Ernst did, however, read Walter Künneth's critique of Rosenberg from the point of view of a more orthodox Christianity, and took it seriously.[61] He would not have been an uncritical disciple of Rosenberg.

On Good Friday 1941 Ernst wrote to Lilo full of enthusiasm about the recent German victories, but focused on Easter as well. "My thoughts flit over to you, and with you to God. God speaks to us in the redeeming death of Jesus on the Cross. Let Jesus's mighty life and superhuman dying lead us to our Father in heaven and rest quietly in God's protective presence."[62]

Faith and patriotism had been inseparable in Ernst's family tradition, a patriotism now infused with National Socialist ideology. As he wrote to Lilo in March 1940, "You know the emotions which always fill my heart.

---

58. Rollin, "'*Gott schuf keine Stände, keine Klassen, aber Rassen.*'"

59. Ernst to Lilo, January 25, 1936.

60. Rosenberg, *Der Mythus des 20. Jahrhunderts*, 629.

61. Ernst to Lilo, November 18, 1936; Künneth is an ambivalent figure: he rejects Rosenberg's anti-Christianity but is himself anti-Semitic. See Künneth, *Antwort auf den Mythus*.

62. *Lassen wir uns durch Jesu gewaltiges Leben und übermenschliches Sterben unserem Vater im Himmel zuführen und stille werden in der Geborgenheit in Gott.* Ernst to Lilo, April 10, 1941.

Why Hitler? Why National Socialism?

We both recognize the holy necessity for perseverance, determination and *Durchbeißens* (grit). Let's throw off all anxiety and set our sights on the great coming Reich of a magnificent German nation. My dearest, 'Forward,' with God's help!"[63] Yet when he informed Lilo in January 1941 that his brother Hans's fiancée, Gerda, was debarred from teaching by a Party official because she stood by her Christian faith, he clearly approved of Hans continuing to stand by her.[64] He was also annoyed by propaganda films such as *Der Frisennot (The Distress of the Frisians)*, which presented the traditional, biblical faith of a German Mennonite community in Russia as unrealistic und muddled.[65] Ernst's confused but emphatic statements no doubt reflect the views of many Protestants at this time.[66]

Lilo was less clear about her religious views, and she admits in an early letter in 1936 that she had not got far beyond her childhood faith. She enjoyed playing the organ and had helped the pastor in Swinemünde with the services for the children, but the Bible was largely a mystery to her. She shared Ernst's identification of faith and patriotism and was furious with the pastor in Spantekow when he failed to give thanks in a service for the Reich's troops marching into the Rhineland in March 1936![67] Her mother prayed fervently for God's help in the conflicts with her husband, but Lilo herself felt she had lost her way as far as prayer was concerned.

She hoped Ernst, who had asked her which her favorite gospel was, could help her. On one occasion she wrote *dass Du in Gott stehst* (that you have God within you).[68] She listed her eleven favorite hymns, including "Jesu geh voran" ("Jesus, Lead Us Forwards").[69] She tended to imagine the worst, though, and glib advice to rest one's confidence in God meant little to her. In her lonely days and nights she wondered what she would do if Ernst were to die, and the very thought of the Russians filled her with horror. She was also concerned about what happens to one after death.

---

63. Ernst to Lilo, March 24, 1940.
64. Ernst to Lilo, January 30, 1941.
65. Ernst to Lilo, February 26, 1936.
66. Countless poems and songs of the time assumed a symmetry of *Gott und Volk* (God and nation), fostering a *frommes, eisernes Geschlecht* (an "unflinching, God-fearing people").
67. Lilo to Ernst, March 7, 1936.
68. Lilo to Ernst, April 12, 1936.
69. Other hymns: "*Wach auf du deutsches Land*"; "*Hinunter ist der Sonne Schein*"; it was the music that spoke to her most, one suspects; Lilo to Ernst, February 23, 1936.

She sometimes talked about the impersonal power of one's *Schicksal* (fate). Ernst detected a certain fatalism in her attitudes, and his response was affectionate but almost stern:

> *Dearest, why are you thinking about what comes after death? That is where faith comes in. . . . Love and hope should bear us up, and faith in our heavenly Father. Put everything in his caring fatherly hands. . . . Dearest, do drop this alarm about the Russians. . . . If you are a loving wife to me, a loyal mother to the children, and a comrade happy to act responsibly for the Volk you will fulfil your duty. There's no point in anxious thoughts. Work and the right attitude is what give form to life. . . . Devotion releases energy.*[70]

She taught her two little children their first prayers. When a neighbor died unexpectedly, she commented that we were all in God's hand and could not escape our fate. Perhaps her throwaway comment about a man who had "hands like a pastor" hints at her sense that the clergy had an easy life of it.[71] She prayed every day for Ernst's safe return. When, evening after evening, her little daughter prayed, "Dear God, keep Daddy safe," Lilo had tears in her eyes.[72]

As winter engulfed the Russian Front, she reflected:

> *This mad war. How much agony it produces. How much prayer, tears, and probably also curses. Every hour our best German blood is shed, and God, who oversees it all, affirms this. I am of the view that blessing can never come of war. All life is God's gift yet now that life is murdered a thousand times over. As a woman I cannot say 'Yes' to this war . . . but nothing can stop it.*[73]

Christmas, the festival of peace, would be meaningless for her in 1941, she feared.[74] The death in battle of Herr von Harniers, a local aristocrat with a young family, hit her very hard. She knew the family well, had enjoyed their hospitality:

> *Nothing happens against God's will, but can it be God's will, all this wretchedness, agony, tears, all this murdering; is all that God's will? Ach, dear Ernst, I don't know what to think. Often it seems to me*

---

70. Ernst to Lilo, April 28, 1941; note his emphasis on duty.
71. Lilo to Ernst, December 9, 1940.
72. Lilo to Ernst, June 30, 1941.
73. Lilo to Ernst, November 15, 1941.
74. Lilo to Ernst, November 29, 1941.

> *impertinent to beseech God to bring you back to us. Why should we be spared when millions must make such sacrifices? Ach, my dearest, it is hard to live in this dreadful world.*[75]

Her pain and confusion would have been shared by many women in her position. She was asking, one feels, many of the right questions. Her church contacts, such as they were, seemed to have offered her little or nothing in the way of dealing with them.

Ernst responded:

> *Your letter of 7 December is at my side. You mention the heroic death of Lt. von Harniers. Yes, my dear, it is heartbreaking to share in these cruel individual tragedies. I myself emerged from such distress and never knew my father. It is beyond words awful to lose one's beloved. I just hope that those whom it befalls are as full of trust in God as my mother was. Nothing was ever made easy for her, yet she remained full of energy and love. . . . How often have we had to be reminded of the saying: 'Where distress is greatest, God is closest'?*
>
> *Which of us, when confronting distress, faced with all the tears and all the murdering, wants to argue with God? We say 'your will be done' and acknowledge his laws. Either we acknowledge God in our distress, bow down in humility and find new strength from him, or fate will roll over us mercilessly. Our prayer touches the depths of God's being. Total surrender is required if it is to give us strength. No calculating and judging, no questioning and speculating, but trusting and believing. Energy generates life. God conferred it on us and we have to reach for it again and again from his hand: energy for love, for action, for living and for dying.*[76]

Total surrender! There was nothing nominal about Ernst's Christianity. It provided the firm personal base to his commitment to the new Germany and to Hitler's wars.

---

75. Lilo to Ernst, December 7, 1941; she reports on the very moving funeral in a packed church; his brave widow was carrying their fifth child.

76. Ernst to Lilo, December 29, 1941.

The Photos

Photographs have a life of their own. Photos are never just illustrations of the text. They tell their own story. We learn from them aspects of reality at which letters or documents can only hint. That is particularly true for the amateurish snapshots taken by and for Lilo and Ernst. They do not begin to compare, technically, with the vast array of superb photographs available about every aspect of the life of the Third Reich. We are well acquainted, if not satiated, with the pomposity and horror of these graphic depictions.

These snapshots are "something else": family photographs, intimate glimpses of the domestic and personal world of Lilo and Ernst. As we know from the letters, they were framed and treasured as representations of the absent one. They took pride of place in Lilo's homes in Wrohm and Spantekow and they were displayed on the walls of Ernst's barrack rooms, his huts, and his dugouts. Like icons, they were revered and kissed.

Their visual quality helped to assuage the tyranny of distance, to evoke not only the face of the partner but to offer evidence that his or her world remained intact, and was not a dream but real. The children were real, Lilo and Ernst were real. The photos were fragments of hopefulness, wisps of promise that their lives would come together again.

The Photos

1. Ernst with Landjahr (Year on the Land) Group. 1935. Family photo.

2. Lilo with BDM (League of German Girls). 1935. Family photo.

3. Lilo and Ernst. 1936. Family photo.

4. Ernst with bike in Wrohm. 1938. Family photo.

The Photos

5. Ernst with Wrohm School children. 1938. Family photo.

6. Ernst. 1939. Family photo.

7 Lilo and Ernst reading. 1939. Family photo.

8. Ernst with daughter, Heinke. 1939. Family photo.

THE PHOTOS

9. Ernst with 'Prince' in France. 1940. Family photo.

10. Ernst back from France, with Heinke. 1941. Family photo.

LOVE AND TERROR IN THE THIRD REICH

11. Ernst, with Heinke. 1941. Family photo.

12. Lilo, Heinke, Ernst. 1941. Family photo.

The Photos

13. Hartmut, Lilo, Heinke. 1941. Family photo.

14. Ernst on the Russian Front. 1942. Photo by fellow-soldier.

15. Heinke, Lilo as widow, Hartmut. 1943. Family photo.

16. Heinke and Hartmut. 1946. Family photo.

4

Russia

What Hitler wanted was the annihilation of the Russian state and nation.... He was probably willing to let the majority of the Russian-speaking people survive, but not as a nation, not as belonging to a state. Anyone, he said, who showed the least bit of opposition, should be shot.

—GOLO MANN, 1958[1]

AFTER HIS TIME IN France and some precious days of leave in Wrohm with the family, Ernst was moved eastwards and was initially stationed in the Polish town of Graudenz, in West Prussia, which despite years of Polish rule, retained a strong German feel, which could be traced back seven hundred years to its foundation by the *Deutscher Orden* (German Order). German troops had marched in there in September 1939, a concentration camp was set up, the Jews were rounded up and shot in the nearby forests, and the Polish intellectuals and one hundred and fifty priests were arrested and many of them killed. When Ernst arrived more than a year later, he lived comfortably in a Polish teacher's home (!) in Blücherstrasse. There is no hint of these atrocities in the steady flow of his positive letters to Lilo, in which he hopes she could come to visit him there, or perhaps in Berlin. Traveling with two young children was really out of the question, however. Ernst found it hard to settle down to military routine again after his leave,

---

1. Mann, *Deutsche Geschichte 1919–1945*, 173 (my translation); Littell, *The Kindly Ones*, 101 is probably unsurpassed as an imaginative depiction of the Russian campaign, with its theme "You must resist the temptation to be human."

and begged Lilo to write as often as possible so that he was kept in close touch. His clamant need for letters is obvious. Much of their correspondence at this time is about practical details: clothes, money, work in the garden, and the inadequacy of the substitute teacher in Wrohm, Herr Meggers.

Yet the cantus firmus of the correspondence was always the strength of their love. "What a lovely life," Lilo wrote in the second year of the war. In two years of marriage they had grown inwardly, and now lived consciously and maturely. "We have merged into one another so fully. I cannot imagine thinking differently from you. To have respect for one's man or woman makes you so superior to those who only want to enjoy life. Our reward is a purer one, high above intellectual drives. One can only give oneself once." Her trust in him was boundless. She marveled at his energy and initiative, the way he reveled in his tasks.[2] "I'll go through thick and thin with you. Suffering and distress with you at my side are not half so bad." She always felt so close to him, though he was far away. "Every evening I sense you right by me, and offer you my love, *mein Butzi* (my darling)."[3]

He was in the 290th Infantry Division, which was partly motorized, and partly dependent on horses; some two-thirds of the division were career soldiers, one-third, like Ernst, were reservists. As the military history of the division (*290. Infanterie Division. Weg und Schicksal*) points out, the fact that it was not wholly motorized meant exhausting forced marches for battalions such as Ernst's.[4]

The Nazi-Soviet pact was still in operation, and Ernst had as little idea as the next man that it was about to be voided. His anxiety, on the contrary, was that the war would be over before he had seen any action. His duties included responsibility for cultural affairs—organizing, for example, an army Day, which included horse rides for the (German) children in Graudenz. Most days were filled with routine training, and some evenings were taken up for the officers with meetings he had to attend, but generally he could use the evenings to listen to the radio, write letters, or do some reading. Every now and then they would go on long forced marches, on occasion getting up as early as half-past-three in the morning.[5] Several letters men-

---

2. Lilo, to Ernst, June 20, 1940; April 23, 1941.

3. Lilo, to Ernst, June 9, 1941; March 17, 1940.

4. Bauer, *290. Infanterie Division. Weg und Schicksal*; the history is detailed and accurate, but its perspectives betray its postwar genesis; the Russian forces are apostrophized as "Iwan."

5. Ernst to Lilo, March 27, 1941.

tion these long, tiring days and hint at his weariness. One even mentions him having to work hard to combat his "depressions."[6]

Together with the usual letters he sent off a sheaf of illustrated postcards for the children, including one for Heinke's second birthday on February 12: "Dear Heinke, your Pappi is thinking of you on your birthday and wishes you 'Good Appetite!' Every happiness in the coming year, a sparkle in your eye and joy in your heart"; then later in the year: "Dear Heinke, dear Hartmut, Pappi is far away from you both, but when he shuts his eyes he is right beside you. Pappi loves you both so very much. When the war is over he will be back with you. Be nice to Mummy always. Your Pappi."[7] He was deeply concerned when the children fell sick or made things difficult for Lilo.

By the second week of April they were on the move eastwards, heading for East Prussia, in long forced marches, in part through the night with only short snatches of sleep. He declined offers from farmers for better food than what his men were eating. The news from Greece and Africa filled him with elation, and he imagined Lilo would feel the same: the war would soon be over, he rejoiced, given the momentum of these advances and the vision of their leadership.[8] He jollied his men along on the marches with singing, which helped them forget their blisters. National Socialist songbooks such as *Wohlauf Kameraden (Forward, Comrades)* explicitly regarded singing as a weapon, a *Kampfruf* (a call to arms). Germany should wake up, shoulder the weapons, hold true to "the old God, the true God," to the Führer, to the Reich, to one's comrades, to freedom. Holding high the flag, knowing there was no more wondrous land than theirs, they would march into a better future.[9]

Ernst himself dismounted and walked with the men. Even the horses were, in his words, admirably loyal. "They pull and bear heavy burdens without protest, and when you speak to them they understand, prick up their ears or stay still. I keep close to them and never lose them out of my sight."[10]

---

6. Ernst to Lilo, April 9, 1941.
7. Ernst to Lilo, undated, probably December 1941.
8. Ernst to Lilo, April 10, 1941; April 13, 1941.
9. Pollmann, ed., *Wohlauf Kameraden!* Ernst's copy dates from his time in Schalkholz.
10. Ernst to Lilo, April 15, 1941.

By April 14, 1941, they had reached East Prussia. The weather could be fickle, with snow showers as late as May, but he enjoyed riding out in the countryside with his horse, Titus, splashing through the rivers, charging down hills, and jumping over barriers. He described in detail the honey, hams, rich soups, and warm hospitality offered him by his East Prussian hosts, the Kretschmanns. They were Catholic, but he managed to keep off any religious themes! Despite the long days and short nights on the way there, he kept the cards and letters flowing homewards, hoping his daughter had fun searching for her Easter eggs, and pouring out his heart to Lilo. He lived for and by her warm letters. When he meditated on the *unfaßbare Allmacht* (indescribable power) of their love, everything trivial was left behind, and he could only thank God for the unbelievable gift he had been given in his wife. He had sixteen photos of her and the children on the wall of his room, smiling down at him.[11] Their love was a complete one; it was so marvelous to have Lilo, not only as a passionate partner in physical love, but as a soul friend. They really understood each other, and their letters reflected this reality. Her pain and tears at their enforced separation did her such credit.[12]

Yet her penchant for melancholy worried him. "Why be fearful and despairing?" He tried to pull her out of her growing depression and weariness with life in Wrohm, which was compounded by the air raids. He emphasized the depth of their love and the cosmic dimensions of Germany's *Weltziel* (its mission in the world). Maybe, he suggested, she should move to her parents' home for a while. If she turned "I must" into "I should," it would help.[13] His favorite concept of duty again!

No doubt he thought that if she moved eastwards, they would then be much nearer to each other when he was given leave. Lilo's father strongly encouraged the idea. (The stamp on one of her father's letters to Ernst depicts Churchill with a sinking warship on his bald pate and, instead of the cost of the stamp, the words: "not worth a cent!")[14]

Everyone was keenly awaiting the Führer's next address, he wrote Lilo in early May 1941. Ernst was sure "the film" (the war) would soon be over. His faith in Germany and in the Führer, like his confidence in Lilo's love, was limitless, and enabled him to rise above "sad thoughts. . . . A hidden fire

---

11. Ernst to Lilo, April 17, 1941; April 19, 1941; May 31, 1941.
12. Ernst to Lilo, April 21, 1941; April 23, 1941.
13. Ernst to Lilo, May 4, 1941; May 18, 1941.
14. Ernst to Lilo, May 9, 1941.

is smoldering just under the surface in some quarters, in others emotions run high and stormy. What lies ahead? Why this hate?" Does he mean hate of Germany? The reference is unclear, but may be to Russia or America.[15]

Letters refer to his depression at the unedifying aspects of military life: being bossed around, ordered to do one thing one minute, having the commands countermanded the next; he summed it up as *das ewige Getretenwerden* (human dignity being trampled underfoot) by *den Herrn Strebern* (arrogant go-getters). The lack of time for reflection and the meaningless activities got him down: "this life as a soldier is the best and shortest way to *geistigem Tod* (intellectual death)."[16] He didn't get on that well with the other officers, and they kept their distance.[17] One would like to know more about this.

In the meantime what he dubbed their "tour group" moved ever further eastwards, sometimes covering sixty kilometers a day. Spring was tardy, and the fields were frosty, even icy in places. He revisited some of the places where he had been working years before in the Landjahr, and enjoyed meeting the farming families again.[18]

By mid-May, when they reached their temporary goal, the little village of Szugken, near Tilsit, they had covered well over five hundred kilometers on foot, often marching through the night. Again the singing helped. Almost overnight the weather then turned very hot.

New to him were the open-air film shows, which he greatly enjoyed. But a surprise meeting with his younger brother, Hans, was the real delight. They met in a little village inn and talked till the cows came home. A fortnight later Hans cycled some twenty-five miles to visit him; they had coffee together, then put on their shorts and set off through the sunny countryside to a little river, the Gollume, where they stripped off "and fooled around in the knee-deep water, splashing one another. It was just great. We then wandered down the riverbed barefoot, singing 'Schon wieder blühet die Linde' ('The Lime Tree Is in Blossom Again')."[19]

By the end of the month they were within four miles of the Russian border. Interestingly the Christian festival of Whitsun was celebrated in

---

15. Ernst to Lilo, May 13, 1941; the reference appears to be to the unpredictability of politics.
16. Ernst to Lilo, May 26, 1941; May 13, 1941; May 24, 1941; May 29, 1941.
17. Ernst to Lilo, May 28, 1941.
18. Ernst to Lilo, May 6, 1941.
19. Ernst to Lilo, May 11, 1941.

style in this German army, with traditional *Kaffee und Kuchen* (coffee and cakes), then champagne and red wines. Ernst rustled up a special pudding, but he remained rather out of sorts, missing home, and fed up with army discipline; he felt "hemmed in" by the responsibility for his thirty-six men, twenty-six horses, and all the equipment. He was infuriated by one of his men, a smart aleck from Berlin, and reluctantly had him disciplined for insubordination. Fortunately he was moved on to another platoon.[20]

The thought of a happy past and a hopeful future cheered him up. In his Whitsun letter Ernst quoted Hermann Claudius: "Man, woman and my children / what a sweet song / accompanying all my ways." He imagined Lilo getting out of bed, combing that hair he loved to bury his face in, and then their going together to look at the sleeping children, and to wander through the garden. His brother, Hans, who had spent Whitsun with Ernst, added a penciled greeting to "dear Lilo and the children."[21]

Lilo was becoming ever more anxious. She became annoyed if Ernst didn't respond to her questions but followed his own train of thought. Ernst's letters do have a rather liturgical, repetitive quality, with snippets of news, assurances that all is well, and professions of his undying love. His reserve may be partly due to Lilo's indiscreet and detailed questions about the next stage of the war. She had heard of mass movements of troops to the east, and of tanks covering huge distances and wanted to know what this meant. Her questions, too, about the length of the war were difficult for him to answer. She wondered why he was so punctilious about the training of his men. Others seemed to take it more cavalierly. Above all she was insistent that he should tell her the unvarnished truth, so that she knew what he had been up against. She didn't want to be protected from it.

She had been badly shaken by graphic reports of the bombing in Hamburg in mid-1941, not least because Ernst's sister, Leni, and other relatives lived there. Her hope for a speedy end to hostilities was rapidly diminishing but a letter from Ernst intimating new initiatives to be launched against Britain bucked her up somewhat:

> *My dear Ernst, your letter did wonders for me and once again my spiritual barometer has risen, because I know that you understood where my anger was coming from and that I was really stressed out. It made me so happy that you write that we are both marching in*

---

20. Ernst to Lilo, June 3, 1941; it is worth mentioning, because generally Ernst got along well with the men.

21. Ernst to Lilo, March 31, 1941; June 1, 1941.

the same direction, and it cheers me up to no end and gives me fresh courage that you believe decisive military actions are imminent. One hears the opposite all the time, and everything is so discouraging. Leni says the same of Hamburg. Elsa Butenschön wrote from Heringsdorff yesterday from the camp of evacuated children; they are settling in for the winter now, installing ovens and central heating. It really shocked me. As far as Hamburg is concerned I know that they are beginning to build massive air raid shelters and that some firms are only now switching to making armaments, and that it will be a year or so before they can go into full-scale production. . . . So you see, it all looks like a lengthy war ahead, doesn't it? The tiny spark of hope that still flickers in one's heart gets snuffed out so quickly. Are you unhappy about my timorous letters; do they make it harder for you to keep going? Am I letting myself go too much, moaning and groaning? It only lasts until things are clarified, and by then one is usually over the worst, isn't one?

We had thunder at night and bombers again for the first time in ages. We're getting into these long bright nights again. These air torpedoes are awesome. They create a huge blast of air. Whole terraces of houses collapse, and attempts to reach the survivors trapped in the ruins are seldom successful. Ernst, can you see any possible sense or Segen (blessing), in such murder? I'd like to be a pacifist, there's a lot to be said for it. May God return you to us safely, my dearest, for the time for your own involvement is nearing; it's too awful for me to contemplate.[22]

She was alarmed by the continual extension of the hostilities to the eastern Mediterranean and Africa. The thought of Ernst going to Greece or even further horrified her.[23] Then as she saw her man marching ever nearer to Russia, she quite rightly deduced that an invasion was imminent, and was petrified at the thought of Ernst being drawn into battle with the Reds.

Ernst continued to protest that there was no danger of hostilities with Stalin. He expected to remain in East Prussia for a considerable time. Why so much alarm about Russia? Her alarm and negativity got under his skin, as did her questions about whether he genuinely wanted to see her and the children again. Tact was never a strong point with Lilo. He was close at times to *loswettern* (a thunderous retort) to such questions, but managed

22. Lilo to Ernst, May 29, 1941.
23. Lilo to Ernst, January 5, 1941.

to restrain himself.²⁴ He attempted to allay her fears, interpreting all the preparations on the Eastern Front as contingency measures.

A letter to Lilo from her brother, Dieter, on June 2, 1941, throws light on the mood within the German army at the time. Dieter was in hospital, recovering from a serious accident on an army motorbike, compounded by a badly strained ankle. He had carried on regardless, however, since German officers ignore such trifles, only to collapse with what was diagnosed as severe pneumonia. He was livid with the doctors who insisted that he stay in bed, because it was clear from all the preparations going around him, injections and so on, that the march into the East was imminent. It was, he feared, his last chance as a young lieutenant. "I have to be part of this."²⁵ It seems inconceivable that Ernst was not equally aware of an imminent attack.

For today's readers, Ernst's combination of sensitivity and affection with apparently uncritical acceptance of National Socialist propaganda is hard to take. Indeed with hindsight, knowing, as we now do, that on June 22, 1941, Operation Barbarossa was about to be launched, the mass of details in Ernst's letters about the meals he was eating, the vegetables and flowers in the Wrohm garden, the occasional naughtiness of the children, or even about Lilo's inflamed eyes could seem like a perverse refusal to look reality in the face. That may well be unfair, however, . Lilo's newsy and affectionate letters did work their magic on him, transporting him into another world, and it is certainly true that he was entranced by every scrap of information about the children: Hartmut falling asleep in the sandpit, the two-year-old Heinke saying her evening prayers. He could not hear enough of this.²⁶

He wrote on the very eve of the invasion of Russia, on June 20, from a camp in the woods, describing the chattering of the finches, the call of a cuckoo, and his men sitting around the open fire in a semicircle drinking beer till midnight, their only problem being the midges. However, the next letter, a whole week later, came from deep within Lithuanian territory. Some hastily written, largely illegible fragments of his diary convey something of the turmoil of these first days of the invasion:

---

24. Ernst to Lilo, May 18, 1941.

25. Dieter to Lilo, June 2, 1941; the letter is typed; in a letter to his mother from the Front on 1 February 1942 he described himself as "the happiest man in the world" in his role as a lieutenant.

26. The official history suggests that most were well aware that an attack was in the offing; Bauer, *290. Infanterie Division. Weg und Schicksal*, 41–42.

> *22.6. 3.05 am, the attack begins. . . . Cross the border . . . 14 riders patrol ahead, Russian planes, German fighters. . . . Sand, sun, heat. Local population offers water, eggs, milk, ham, cheese.*
>
> *Why? Completely exhausted; fall asleep on horse. Nonsense. Quarters requisitioned. . . . Communists taken captive. . . . In many villages, swastika and Lithuanian flags flying. . . . Two days of rain as move towards Dünaburg. Pass through Dünaburg, destroyed Russian tractor and field guns.*[27]

The news of the invasion of Russia in June was a terrible blow for Lilo, because she knew now that Ernst could soon be in mortal danger. Any faint hopes she had had for a quick termination to the war now vanished. Russia shouldn't have happened.[28] She knew that it was Ernst's dearest wish to fight for his country, but the letter in which she responded to the news about Russia collapses at the end into emotional disarray. One senses the tears in her eyes as she puts pen to paper.

> *My most beloved man, dear, dear Ernst, loving father of our children. Today your letter of the 21st arrived. At long last, the weight is lifted from my heart and I can write again. If I only knew how you are doing, and where you are positioned. I've already written several letters since the 22nd. The days and the nights are pure torture, this crazy tension just tears at my nerves. I dare not think too much about all these dreadful events. The most dear person in the world to me in danger! If only my great love could preserve you. Be assured that I am with you night and day and pray God to keep you safe for me and the children. Are you still well, free of wounds, my dearest? How are you coping with all these hardships? Please, please, send me a sign of life. I telephoned Father to ask him to join me straight away, but unfortunately he can't make it till 13 July. I can't bear it on my own.*
>
> *I was sure war in Russia was in the cards and when the news came on Sunday morning it was ein Schlag ins Gesicht (an awful shock). My heart sank, for I knew you would be involved in the invasion. I heard on the report from the Front that the attack in the north was made without artillery, relying on heavy infantry weaponry. I assumed that you are charging up the Baltic and seeking to link up with Finland. Nothing about that in the army reports, only that there will be a Sondermeldung (a special proclamation) tomorrow. It's said that the war is treacherous, worse than in Poland.*

---

27. Ernst to Lilo, June 18, 1941.
28. *Rußland hätte nicht kommen dürfen.* Lilo to Ernst, September 3, 1941.

> *I dare not think about it; did you manage to get the photos of the children? How good if they could be a talisman on your way.*
>
> *Your yearning to be part of the action has now been fulfilled, dear Ernst. I wish you every good fortune as a soldier, so that you come back home safely. Don't worry about us. Everything is fine, we are well, and our only concern is for you. The two years of separation don't count any more. I will gladly wait as long as it takes if in the end my dear, young man is back with us again. My love knows no limits, not even that of death.*
>
> *I have to stop now, my beloved, I can't go on. I will write each day; my prayers are with you. The dear little ones send you a big kiss. Words can't express what I am feeling. I am always, always your dear Lilowife. Dieter has a new field post number 02899A. Tudi, Robert and family are with Mother. Please, please, a card to assure me you're alive.*[29]

Two days later, she sent off another letter in similar vein. She followed, of course, the *Sondermeldungen*, the bombastic announcements of victories in Russia, which interrupted the normal radio program, but was soon heartily sick of them. She couldn't face any more talk of heavy fighting. Her first thought was of all that German blood being shed.

From the point of view of the National Socialist Party, Lilo was selfishly focused on the individual welfare of her own family, and indeed she was exceedingly fortunate that the increasingly forceful complaints she voiced in her letters about the war did not attract the attentions of the military censor. Anything viewed as destructive to national solidarity and morale the Party and the State took with utmost seriousness as *Wehrkraftzersetzung* (undermining the men at the Front).[30] Illustrated pamphlets warned women against writing pessimistic letters to their menfolk. Soldiers had enough to cope with fighting the enemy and did not need to be further burdened with needless fears and complaints.[31]

Although she was dependent on the narrow range of information provided by the media, she measured pronouncements and slogans by the reality she encountered day by day, by the death notices in the paper, and by her conversations with others, especially other wives who had men at the

---

29. Lilo to Ernst, June 28, 1941.

30. Defeatist utterances could attract the most draconian penalties under the *Kriegssonderstrafrechtsverordnung (Special Criminal Code for the War)* of 1938.

31. One such pamphlet is headed this way: *Verzagte Briefe schreibt man nicht; Die Front erwartet Zuversicht*, and it portrays a sobbing woman writing a letter, and a deeply upset soldier having to read it.

Front. She had her own personal networks. For all her naivety and limited information, her intuition about the direction of events was sounder than that of her husband, though as the campaign ground on, the determination and depth of the Russian resistance astonished her.[32]

A card from Ernst on June 27, reporting that he already had advanced some hundred and fifty kilometers, confirmed that there had been no enemy contact, and that only German planes were flying overhead. A quite detailed letter on the same day described the forced marches through the night, with at times only three hours' sleep, grabbing a bite to eat while continuing to march, and then seeing to the watering of the horses. The heat was oppressive, the dust so bad on the poor, sandy roads that sometimes you couldn't even see the person in front of you. As a tank division pushed ahead, the infantry sprawled out on their stomachs by the side of the road, and he had a chance to write the letter. The lack of any Russian resistance meant that the campaign felt like a maneuver.[33]

They had been able to go for a swim in a lake, a real delight. He was struck initially by the fruitfulness of the land, which made him think of Lilo and the children enjoying the strawberries in Wrohm. The people lived in stinking, wooden hovels, though, and the women ran around barefoot. The poverty was grim, with few owning more than a cow or a few hens, most of the land having been collectivized. The people hated the Reds.[34]

The German troops obviously preferred their tents to such poor accommodation. After about a week on the go they were back to regular times for sleep and meals. He was greatly impressed by the efficiency of the supply lines. Of their food he mentioned bacon, cheese, tinned fish, honey, and tins of gooseberries. The real fighting was being done by the advance columns with their tanks. They were fabulous. All the infantry could do at this point was to follow them, at a distance of about sixty kilometers, and occupy the land. However, Ernst mentioned seven fatalities in his company of two hundred men. The only Russian troops they had seen were prisoners.

His letters offer little cameos of army life: the men caring for the horses, cleaning their rifles, and listening to the radio; if anything it was all a tad boring. Soldiers, though, took life as it came, and relished every chance to rest up. Every letter chanted such litanies of reassurance to Lilo.[35]

32. Lilo to Ernst, August 12, 1941.
33. Ernst to Lilo, June 27, 1941; July 9, 1941.
34. Ernst to Lilo, July 27, 1941.
35. In her novel about generational conflict after the war, Ulla Hahn points out that

As a young officer, Ernst was concerned for the welfare of his men, and enjoyed leading his platoon: "the men hold by me. The relationship is what I had always dreamed of."[36] He emphasized that he himself was fit and well.

He pictured to himself the little family in Wrohm. The misery he saw around him alerted him to how privileged their life at home was in comparison. Then a footnote: Lilo should please look up the marriage documents of their parents, as Ernst and she were required to prove their Aryan descent.[37]

By July 10, 1941, they were into Russia itself, the "Red Paradise," encountering little but desolation and deserted villages, a burnt-earth policy having been adopted by the enemy on its own land and people. But the countless lakes had the troops stripping off, bathing, and lying around naked or in their shorts, lapping up the sun. Ernst opened a bottle of liqueur in honor of his happy memories of his last leave and shared it around. He wrote his letters sitting on a rug on the ground. There was a shortage of paper, and writing on one's knees was tricky, but he was getting there![38]

As he began to receive her letters, Ernst was puzzled and perturbed by Lilo's perceptible distress and worry on his behalf. "I am in the hands of a higher power, and trust Him. . . . Tanned and toughened up we go forwards. My dearest, our sacrifice, with that of so many others, is ensuring a new world. Onwards with God for Germany!"

They were steadily advancing in a northeasterly direction through the endless plains with their fields of corn, vast forests, and moorland, apparently heading for Staraja Russa in the Novgorod region. Some of the villages were deserted, but not all.[39] The main crops were potatoes, peas, barley, and corn. The inhabitants, once they overcame their shyness, welcomed them and cursed Communism, and gave them milk and water. The children played around their tents.

Ernst seemed unconscious of the irony of reporting about friendly inhabitants while being amused by the troops chasing down geese and roasting them. The houses of the inhabitants resembled nothing so much

---

it was very much military policy, as the *Mitteilungen für die Truppe* (*Information for Frontline Troops*) made clear: letters home should be "manly," positive, free of all doubts about the aims of the Führer. Field post should strengthen the morale of the home front; Hahn, *Unscharfe Bilder*, 74.

36. Ernst to Lilo, May 16, 1941.
37. Ernst to Lilo, July 1, 1941; July 3, 1941; July 4, 1941; July 9, 1941.
38. Ernst to Lilo, July 10, 1941; July 11, 1941
39. Ernst to Lilo, July 17, 1941; July 19, 1941.

as miserable cattle sheds.[40] When they reached Staraja Russa, which had been heavily shelled, his heart went out to the wretched civilians who had fled to the woods and made dugouts for themselves, but who were virtually starving.[41] A month later he and other riders stumbled across a group of women and children who had been driven out of the town (and whose homes were now occupied by the Germans), and who were trying to eke out an existence in clay huts in the middle of the forest. All unbelievably primitive.[42]

The incredible speed of the initial advance made Lilo wonder if she'd see him back by August after all. However, until she got the first letters from him from the East on July 4, she was in an agony of fear from dawn to dusk. Her neighbors in Wrohm had all noticed it. Her relief was incredible when the letters did begin to arrive.[43] She set off for a brief visit to Spantekow to her parents, and her father reciprocated with a visit to Wrohm.

But then her whole life in Wrohm imploded after a bombing raid on July 21, 1941. Without consulting Ernst, she fled eastwards to her parents' home in Spantekow in Pomerania. As she wrote to Ernst:

> *We are all right, God has preserved us. It was so ghastly that I can scarcely describe it. We thought it was our last day on earth. Providentially Father had arrived in the evening at 8.30 p.m. with a car from Rendsburg. I had been greatly looking forward to it, and we sat and chatted until 11 p.m. I went off to bed so peacefully.*
>
> *I hadn't yet fallen asleep when three bombs made us leap out of bed. We held one another's hands and were still shaking, but thought, 'well it's all over now.' Then the siren went, and we again jumped out of bed. Threw on some things and my first thought was to see to the blackout.[44] We went into the front room, and saw the street, bright as day, with flames lighting everything up, the whole sky glowing red. People raced past yelling: 'Air raid!' Father kept shouting, 'Get away from that window!' but I had to see to the blackout, and the noise of the planes was by then fading off into the distance. Went on to see to the blackout in the kitchen and the dining room. The children were still sleeping. We went to them and just at that moment three bombs came howling down right close to us. We lay on the floor. Then with*

40. Ernst to Lilo, July 23, 1941.
41. The exact date of this letter in August 1941 is uncertain.
42. Ernst to Lilo, September 11, 1941.
43. Lilo to Ernst, July 4, 1941.
44. Lilo is referring to seeing that the windows were covered with dark curtains (blackout curtains) as protection during the air raid.

a child in our arms, wrapped in a blanket, both of us rushed down to the cellar.

There we heard more and more bombs, some twenty-six in all. We perched on the piles of coke, and thought every bomb would be our last. That terrifying howling of the bombs is something I'll never forget. We tucked in our heads, clasped the little ones to us and all we could say was: 'Dear God, save us.' Soon neither of us could say a word, for our mouths were completely dry; we moved our lips but nothing came out. This went on for about 50 minutes. The lights went out, because the power lines in the village were on fire.

Then someone knocked on the house door. It was Granny Doose. I went out with her; the street was abuzz with dark figures. The planes had gone. We began to hear reports of what had happened. Everyone was still shaking, and most were crying. . . . Ambulances arrived, five doctors etc. First we heard that no one was dead, till Buhmann [the taxi driver] came into the village and said that there are people lying out at the back. And there they found the dead and the injured. . . .

Several houses were hit by the seven incendiary bombs, and the people ran out, as they didn't know how to start extinguishing the flames. . . . At least 20 houses. And the poor wretches ran right into the path of the bombs. Three were instantly killed, and were laid out in the school. Among them a ten-year-old little girl from Kiel, who lost both her legs; she lived for five hours. Hans Messer was cut in two. Frau Stolley likewise. Many are still in a critical state in the hospital. Cows and calves are dead. The cries of man and beast were just awful.

[Twenty-six] explosive bombs and more than 200 incendiary bombs had fallen. It was deliberate, because first five or six flares lit up the village, then came the incendiary bombs and, as the flames began to take hold, the explosive bombs followed. Many houses had to be demolished. When the doors jammed, people were trapped and had to smash open the doors with an axe.

We have seen death face to face, and I swore I would leave the place with the children immediately. I am absolutely committed to handing over the children to you unscathed. According to the commission and the district council, more attacks are in the cards, because of the mock airfield at Dellstedt.

Lilo then described the rush to pack their clothes and personal things, the overcrowded trains from Rendsburg, full of evacuees, the frightful journey with luggage and the little ones. She was glad to have arrived in Spantekow, though vegetables and fruit were scarce and dear there. She hated

Russia

leaving Wrohm, and her wonderful, productive garden. But there was no alternative. Her nerves were shot to pieces. The reception in Spantekow was not particularly cordial, either; the children were too disruptive for her mother. She soon realized she would have to move to Swinemünde, though there were to be bomb alarms there too.[45]

In early August Ernst's time for writing was limited, though he did not explain why that was the case, only apologizing that he could only send off postcards. It is clear that his battalion was increasingly involved in heavy fighting. "I am fond of my rifle," is a stray, illuminating comment from this time. He talked of disturbed nights but gave Lilo no details. Heavy rain had forced him to abandon his tent for one of the larger wooden homes. One had to climb up a winding flight of steps to the living room, which was divided into four areas, above and below which was storage space. Thousands of flies buzzed around. They slept on straw on the floor.

Food was still adequate; he mentioned pea soup, bean soup, and lentil soup; vegetables were in short supply. Occasionally a hare would find its way into the pot. The bread ran out quickly. He was conscious of losing out on life's gentler aspects, of becoming more "primitive," and feared he would be repulsive to her, and need her gentle hand to restore him to civilian life when it was all over. He longed to return home, and his heart was always with her. But he would do his duty gladly.

His brother, Hans, was in hospital with a wounded arm, but soon returned to duty. As he had in France, Ernst made an effort to learn the local language, but found Russian difficult. Not many officers, one suspects, took the trouble to do this.[46] They moved for a short time from village life to the heavily destroyed town of Staraja Russa, just south of the Ilmensee; on August 18 he told Lilo that he had been awarded the Iron Cross.[47] A letter four days later talked interestingly of many Russian deserters, and of the local population welcoming them as liberators from the discipline of the Soviet commissars.

Ernst was very upset when he heard what Lilo had been through in Wrohm. "My darling," he wrote on August 11:

> *Today your letter of 21 July arrived. Thank you. I can't stop thinking about these awful hours that you, all my dear ones, had to go*

---

45. Lilo to Ernst, July 21, 1941.

46. Ernst to Lilo, August 10, 1941; August 11, 1941; Dieter was soon to be wounded, too, and Hans for a second time, but not seriously.

47. Ernst to Lilo, April 18, 1941.

through. I'm so grateful that you emerged unharmed and are now safe and sound.

Hans [Ernst's brother] was wounded and his lower arm is being treated in the field hospital. He's been awarded the Iron Cross, Second Class. I'm fine. We're still staying in a Russian log house; just moved into a new one. I send my warmest love.

Such a pity that the post is so slow. You'll have received mail from me, though, in the meantime. How are you? Are you recovering, my sweetie? In my thoughts I'm always with you all.[48]

Ernst appeared unperturbed, though, by Lilo's decision to leave Wrohm. He had, after all, suggested as much himself. He loved teaching, but found that the narrow cultural world of the village cramped his style. He wondered where Providence would eventually lead him, what his *Berufung* (true calling) would be.[49] By the beginning of 1941, now an officer in the army, it is clear that Ernst wanted to move on from Wrohm, and to leave primary-school teaching, perhaps for the new *Nachwuchsschulen* (elite schools) for promising pupils.[50] At times Lilo also felt isolated in these Dithmarschen villages in Schleswig-Holstein, and would have been happier nearer the center of the Reich. He was grateful for Lilo's loving letters with all the news about the children. How good that they could go swimming in the Baltic. He himself longed for a proper bath. It was beginning to get quite nippy, he wrote in late August, but they had enough blankets and woolen clothes. However, he was highly indignant at another officer, Telzerow, whose accounts of heavy fighting, fatalities, and *Greuel* (atrocities) had been relayed to Lilo by Telzerow's wife. What a poltroon, what a no-hoper, to relay such stuff to the Home Front! Ernst was dismissive of the whole family. His wife, who was a city slicker, ran the roost at home, and their boy was out of control. Lilo should ignore her; indeed he was soon to ask her to break off all contact with Frau Telzerow.[51] It is not clear what Telzerow meant by "atrocities"; it appears from Ernst's response that it could refer to the grim scenes in field hospitals; but the treatment of Russian civilians could also be meant, which included burning down whole villages when partisan activity was suspected.

---

48. Ernst to Lilo, August 11, 1941.
49. Ernst to Leni, January 20, 1936.
50. Ernst to Lilo, February 5, 1941.
51. Ernst to Lilo, August 22, 1941; August 24, 1941; Lieutenant Hans Telzerow, who gained the Iron Cross but died at the Front on January 25, 1943, at the age of twenty-nine.

RUSSIA

For the first time a letter on August 25, 1941, gave Lilo a relatively detailed picture of the hostilities. Ernst had waited till the fighting was over so she would not worry too much.

> *My dearest. I've just been rereading your letters. As always they warm and strengthen my heart. I am keenly aware of the worries that plague you day and night, but it makes me all the more conscious of your love, which bears me up and to which I keep returning when the Lord God leads me safely through all the dangers.* [This whole sentence underlined in red by Lilo.]
>
> *We have now reached a point after Staraja Russa, where, it seems, we come to a halt. Leningrad and Moscow have to be taken before we resume the advance. For the moment, then, it looks like a break for us. That feels quite strange. For weeks we've bedded down, marched, and eaten the enemy fire. First the heavy fighting at Seebesch, in which Lieutenant Böttger died and our sergeant was wounded. I was in charge of the third platoon, then, in which two men were wounded. We will never forget the murderous artillery fire there. Then we pressed forward, caught up in a succession of battles, at Aleksino facing attacks from bombers and coping with minefields. From the beginning of August there was tense struggle day after day until now. We will never forget places like Sabolotje, Stilina, Garisha, Tschirikowa, Marfina, Michalkino, and especially Staraja Russa. As I mentioned before, I now lead the fourth company, the heavily armed one with 15 cm guns. So far we lost one man, Private Tribien, whose father is a pastor in Hamburg; three men were lightly wounded. Three horses were killed.*
>
> *My horse, Titus, moved from the third to the fourth company with me. He is in great form. The Russian clover makes him nice and fat. He is still full of energy. But I've seldom been out riding these last weeks. You can hit the ground faster if you're on your feet and often the artillery is ahead of us. In Staraja Russa we and our B stand (B squad) were up in the church tower with the artillery. Bullets and shells were flying everywhere! In a brief moment of respite, Kreft, who now heads up the company, presented me with the Iron Cross. All the houses around us were on fire and we returned the Russians' shells with our own greetings.*
>
> *Then came something quite new for us. German bombers and Stukas, up to then scarcely ever seen, smashed the Russians to smithereens. More than 700 were captured, even more killed, so that now we can breathe again. So you can sleep easy now, my dearest, and when Leningrad and Moscow are in our hands I think leave will be the order of the day. Ach, how wonderful that will be! I can't begin to*

imagine it. I think I'll sleep nonstop for a week to begin with, though I'll need a bath first, to dispel the odors of Russia. We are scarcely human any more in this filth.

It does look as if we won't advance beyond the area we've already taken. I think we'll hold the line: Petersburg, Moscow, Kiev–Crimea above the Black Sea, and will leave the clearing up of the other territories to the White Russians. The Russian army is annihilated, so it's just a matter of cleaning up. . . .

Buy whatever you need for yourself, for the children, too. Splash out on clothes, underclothes, stockings and so on. And please buy yourself an amber necklace, my lass, but with my money, eh? My Lilo, you wrote that you'd taken photos, please send them to me, won't you? It would make me so happy. . . . Greetings to everyone at Swinemünde, and give the little ones a kiss from their Daddy. Would you like, maybe, to buy a rose for Grandpa Struck's grave from the 300 DM and give the aunts a present? And please buy a few flowers and give them to Aunt Lisbeth and Aunt Martha with my good wishes.[52]

No doubt it was his leadership in these weeks that earned Ernst the Iron Cross.

Ernst described in detail the village they were in. A creek ran through it, with gardens around each house, and forest on all sides. Newspaper served as wallpaper. No rats or mice, though! It was beginning, as September crept on, to be quite cold and wet, with a real chill in the air, though the sun came out during the day; several of Ernst's men had come down with diarrhea. (One imagines the poor devils at the crude latrines.) He hated the dirt and the pervasive stink. For eleven weeks they hadn't been able to change their clothes. For Ernst this must have been horrendous. He summed up Russia as *trostlos* (bleak and miserable).

He was quite observant about the landscape and village life. Like everyone else he was struck by the endless stretch of the steppes. "The forest dominates the landscape. Firs, pines, birches, beeches, and countless ash trees grow beside one another. Roads, pathways, and cuttings dissect the forest but none of the roads are firm and good." The villages followed the windings of the streams, and the roads were muddy and difficult for vehicles and walkers to negotiate. The houses themselves were roughly built log cabins, accessed by a winding stairway. A thin partition separated kitchen and living room. Bread was baked and food cooked on the same fireplace. The pots were lowered onto the fire, or hung above it.

52. Ernst to Lilo, August 25, 1941.

Russia

Though the Soviet red star was to be found everywhere, most houses also had Christian symbols—little altars and crucifixes hanging in the corner. There was generally a hand-operated grain mill in the cellar. There were no shops in these villages. It was a very elemental economy, everyone doing their own baking or slaughtering. The stalls for the animals were unbelievably dirty and smelly. Potatoes were the main crop in the gardens, together with gherkins, onions, cabbage, and beetroot.[53]

Ernst continued to enjoy robust good health, but asked for various items unobtainable in Russia: a fountain pen, writing paper, also for cigarettes and a pipe. Clearly he had a sweet tooth as sweets, honey, and a cake, if possible, were added to the list. He longed too for some magazines. He made clear his appreciation of Lilo's little parcels of goodies.

As usual, though, he was much more concerned about her well-being. Had she regained weight? He had been shocked that she was down to 108 pounds. That was catastrophic. And how were the toothache and the sore thumb that made writing difficult?[54]

Spantekow, of course, had been Lilo's home as a child, and her being there brought back memories for him of their time there when they were first engaged, of her bedroom, still reminiscent of her days as a young girl, of the warm stove in the living room, and of their delight in each other. He imagined the children playing with their grandfather and enjoying the new environment. Very much the teacher, he also reflected on their two-year-old, Heinke, who would be developing her vocabulary, expanding her understanding of the world, and hopefully learning to play on her own. Knowing how difficult Lilo's mother was, he urged Lilo to bite her tongue and avoid conflict if possible.

The miserable conditions of the war, and the loss of comrades in battle, all this had sharpened Ernst's appreciation of life in peacetime. Faith, hope, and love, the Pauline trio, were what kept him going. Their recent Russian prisoners were raw recruits, poorly equipped, without machine guns and little artillery, so Lilo shouldn't worry.[55] Again and again, we hear this plea. Of course there were fatalities. Of course they were grim sights in the field hospitals. But it was a basic mistake to let worry eat one up. Lamentation of this sort was "un-German."[56] He would never regret participating in this

---

53. Ernst to Lilo, September 7, 1941.
54. Ernst to Lilo, August 28, 1941.
55. Ernst to Lilo, September 2, 1941.
56. Ernst to Lilo, September 5, 1941; September 6, 1941.

momentous campaign. It was the fulfilment of his dreams. Facing death at the Front was something he would not have wanted to miss; he would count it as one of the greatest experiences if his life.[57]

It is hard, though, to know how the average soldier or officer in Ernst's battalion thought about the dangers they faced: the likelihood of death or dreadful injuries leading, for example, to amputation. In the heat of battle there was no time for reflection. Solidarity with their comrades kept them going from day to day, but the strain was often intolerable. A fragment from an undated letter reads: "Dear and faithful God, may I not perish in this wild *Völkerringen* (clash of nations), but lead me home to wife and child, yet your will be done." It was not in Ernst's hand, and did not come from his battalion.[58] It may reflect, though, what many, on both sides of the battle, were going through.

While Ernst was expecting to hear any day of the fall of Stalingrad, Lilo desperately hoped that the Russian campaign would not drag on into the winter. She would be thankful to God her whole life long if he returned safely. She related to him a dream of hers that he had appeared back home before her large as life.[59] His first duty, she felt, ought to be to his young family. She made repeated pleas to him to avoid unnecessary risks. She heartily disliked his practice of riding alone through the woods on his motorbike, or on his horse, exposing himself, she feared, to the risk of snipers.[60] Long after the proposal that he be seconded back to teaching in the *Aufbauschule* (Intensive School) was rejected, she kept coming back to it.[61]

Increasingly a note of desperation is apparent in her letters. It was not just that she was temperamentally less optimistic than Ernst. In her loneliness she saw much more clearly than he did, surrounded as he was by his comrades in arms, that their intact world had been shattered. Despite her love and respect for Ernst, she questioned his judgement about a speedy end to the Russian campaign, and feared above all that his name would soon be being added to the list of fatalities.[62]

Ernst brought up religious arguments in response. Why despair? With trust in God we will cope with these heavy challenges. "There's nothing we

57. Ernst to Lilo, September 8, 1941; Lilo underlined in red the references to fulfillment and to death.

58. Undated; it was with Dieter Struck's papers, but its provenance is unknown.

59. Lilo to Ernst, June 30, 1941; September 7, 1941.

60. Lilo to Ernst, September 20, 1941.

61. Lilo to Ernst, June 12, 1941.

62. Lilo to Ernst, August 17, 1941.

can do about death, for our hour is predestined, and I have faith that I will see you again." The more energy one put into the present, the better despair and *Anfechtung* (anxiety) would be banished. She should throw herself into activity, be a loving mother to the children, as of course she was, and go to sleep thinking of him and entrusting everything to God in prayer. Her despair made it harder for everyone else to tough it out. Leningrad would be in German hands at any moment. He wished with all his heart that he could return to comfort her in person.[63]

He tried his hardest to assure her that his love for her and the children and his sense of duty to his country were in balance:

> *My dearest. My fingers are unusually clean and soft from the washing. I've just come in from hanging out the washing. I hung it up on the big oven for baking and cooking in the 'kitchen.' It's six o'clock and the sun has vanished from the overcast sky. It's getting dark already and I'll have to hurry up with this letter if I'm to finish it today. It's hopeless writing by candlelight. You just ruin your eyes.*
>
> *Sweetie, your last letters from the 26th, 27th and 29th have arrived. Ach, how lovingly you write. You know, of course, how much I look forward to mail from you. Your letter for my birthday also arrived on time. Now and then the post goes so slowly, but this time it was quite quick. Many thanks, my beloved, for your good wishes and your heartfelt hope that we will soon be together again, running our life and bringing up our children. Yes, my Lilo, so far we have been able to draw energy from our memories and dream into our future. You paint so nicely the picture of how the two of us can enjoy that happiness. Thanks to you it is mine; as I settle down to sleep each night I am with you.*
>
> *My sweetie, you're right, we all are heartily sick of the war, and I would be so delighted if I could return to my family circle and devote myself to the school. But my dearest, I will never regret being part of this greatest of all campaigns* [underlined in red by Lilo]. *I know that I would today say the same as I did back then with Granpa Johannsen. I have not changed my mind, my dear, but have had my wish fulfilled. I wouldn't want to miss this commitment, these hardships, looking at death face-to-face* [again underlined]. *This war will rate as one of the greatest experiences in my life, though that doesn't exclude my longing for my dear wife and my little children. I yearn endlessly for you but nevertheless I carry out my duty joyfully* [underlined], *because we are fighting here out of conviction and it's*

---

63. Ernst to Lilo, September 6, 1941; Lilo underlined in red the references to death.

this strong will that enables one to overcome the hardships. That's how I see it.

For the moment we've had a break from the fighting for several days. I've already written you about this, and am particularly pleased for your sake that the battle for Staraja Russa is past history now. My dearest, may I ask you not to meet with Frau Tetzerow. She is not good company, to my mind. I wrote about her once before. Are you still in touch with Elsa Butenschön? Couldn't you meet her some time? Maybe she could come to Spantekow?

My dear, that rumor about troop movements has a real basis. Two divisions are being considered, ours one of them. The other has already been withdrawn. My Lilo can you send me again pictures, photos, and please return Pastor Krause's good wishes? Don't worry about the cigarettes. I'm delighted if you manage to send some, but if not I'll get them here. Today some were available for a change. We could buy 50. It's great if you could get cigarette papers. Borrowing a pipe is quite a business. For the soldier a pipe ranks higher than God. You wouldn't believe it, but it becomes part of him. I have one now. One of my comrades was sent one and he gave it to me. Sweetie, your finger won't heal? You must be using it too much, my lass. It's the thumb, isn't it? I hope it gets better soon.

Sweetie, what are you jabbering about feeling old and faded? How many years do you imagine you'll have to wait? Hoppla, my lass, I've got blood in my veins still. I'll soon drive the wilting out of you. Come, sit on my knee, you dear, sweet little mouse. I kiss you in deepest love, my dear, little Lilofrau. Your Ernst.[64]

There was, however, at the moment no possibility of leave. In the lull in the fighting his life, he wrote, was one of stupefying boredom: eating, sleeping, reading, writing, playing cards, riding out on his horse, and waiting, always waiting. He celebrated his birthday on September 13 by reading again and again her warm and loving birthday letter to him, and imagining every aspect of the family's life in Spantekow. "I conjure up every day the pictures of home."[65] Partly to relieve this monotony he engaged his men in building a new and attractive block house as a refuge in the winter.

A dominant concern in Ernst's letters had always been to reassure Lilo, and to paint a positive picture of his situation in Russia. He had mentioned the initial welcome to the German troops by the Russian villagers and reported on the initial mass attacks by poorly armed Russians, which

---

64. Ernst to Lilo, September 8, 1941.

65. *Ich zaubere mir täglich die Heimatbilder vor Augen.* Ernst to Lilo, September 13, 1941.

had been easily repulsed. Other accounts confirm this. He described how large numbers of Russian troops had come forward to surrender, waving white banners, and after being conducted through the minefields excitedly shook the hands of their captors as they surrendered.[66] A fortnight later he reported on a social occasion with the local population, German soldiers playing music and singing, and the Russians dancing and singing.[67]

Ernst's affectionate letters often did have a healing and comforting effect on his anxious wife. He recalled how her bold, cheeky laughter had utterly won him over. He tried to assure her that his enjoyment of the comradeship of his men, his commitment to Germany and its Führer, and his deep sense of duty were all undergirded by the joy he felt in her and the family. It was for them that he stood at the Front. "Where would I be without you and the dear children?"[68] His longing to return to her was such that he would walk all the way home if he could. He assured her again and again that he understood very well that she must feel felt lonely and depressed. He was sure he would get leave soon, and they could talk everything through and be their old selves again.[69]

Yet their perspectives were drifting apart. Ernst saw the war in Social Darwinist terms, as *Auslese* (a selection of the best). Lilo feared that the contrary could well be true: that it was the best who would perish.[70] Ernst's motto was: "If you keep cheerful, everything is easier." He hoped that the Russians would see sense and capitulate at Stalingrad and avoid its inevitable destruction.[71] He reported an enjoyable sing-along with another platoon. They had sung canons, love songs, soldiers' songs, traditional *Landsknechtslieder* (ballads of the sixteenth-century mercenaries).[72] The whole campaign in the East was going well: "Isn't it great that there is a good chance that it will be all over before winter sets in? Everything has been planned in such a genial and utterly resolute way. . . . These successes were a reward for all the privations and exertions and filled the soldiers

66. Ernst to Lilo, October 26, 1941; it is hard to read this, knowing the wretched fate of most of these prisoners.

67. Ernst to Lilo, November 11, 1941.

68. Ernst to Lilo, October 8, 1941; he offered her detailed advice about disciplining the children; occasionally the stick could be used, but consistency was key, and teaching them that their actions had consequences. Ernst to Lilo, October 13, 1941.

69. Ernst to Lilo, October 11, 1941.

70. Lilo to Ernst, November 23, 1941.

71. Ernst to Lilo, August 8, 1941; September 1, 1941.

72. Ernst to Lilo, October 26, 1941.

with pride." And though confidence in their leaders was firm as a rock, it was great to have such abundant evidence of success.[73]

Such reassurances eventually led, however, to a quite almighty explosion of anger and despair from Lilo. She had deplored the way the war was dragging on. He had replied: "Yes, I understand, but only victory will make our future secure. Our own little life has to be seen in that larger context. . . . The way to victory goes steadily, unerringly forward."[74] Then, in a misplaced attempt to show her how secure and comfortable he was, he described in successive letters how he had built with his men, during a lull in the hostilities, a blockhouse in the forest. What a boost in morale this had been to them all. It was just magnificent!

"Our house in the forest is complete. You should see it." Having sweated over it, they were really proud of the outcome. With its straw-covered roof it would protect them from the wet and the cold. With its small windows it might not look particularly prepossessing, but the main aim had been achieved, to keep out the fierce winds of the Russian winter. Sheep's wool had been packed into any gaps in the timberwork. The stonebuilt stove was a particular success. The cupboards, the cooking arrangements, and the sleeping spaces for himself and the men were described in loving detail. It was comfortable and homely, furnished partly with materials plundered from the Russians. He described how they ate by firelight, the flickering flames lighting up their faces. It felt like something out of Karl May, out of the American Wild West.[75] When he rode out into the forest, its leaves now coloring up as autumn moved towards its height, he now knew he had a cozy home to return to.

This romantic blockhouse was the last straw for Lilo. We have to remember that while he was building for himself this "fairy tale castle," as he dubbed it, she had been compelled to leave her beloved home in Wrohm, and faced an uncertain welcome from a difficult mother in Spantekow. He was surrounded by comrades while she felt deserted and alone:

73. Ernst to Lilo, October 8, 1941.

74. *Herzlieb, es gibt doch nur eins: siegen! Nur ein Sieg kann uns die Unterlage für ein künftiges Leben geben. Das größere ist wichtiger als unser kleines Leben. Sei gewiß, wir schaffen es, und das ist doch die Hauptsache. Du meinst, es ginge langsamer, als man annahm. Ich glaube kaum, dass man mit einem schnellen Sieg rechnete. Die Weite [?] mußaber langsam überwunden werden. Stetig und unbeirrt geht der Weg zum Siege.* Ernst to Lilo, September 26, 1941.

75. Ernst to Lilo, September 22, 1941; September 24, 1941; on 19 October, however, he had to report his fury that they had been ordered to move on, and their fine house now stood empty in the woods.

> *It's been a tough day, my dear Ernst [she wrote]. I've hardly ever known such churning within me. You could never have suspected that it's you and your most recent letters which have precipitated this, especially today's long one of 28 September. It has made me more and more aware that your present situation has you completely contented, that you lack nothing, find everything excellent, and feel happy as Larry!*[76] *You wouldn't want anything to change: in quiet moments you probably still yearn for wife and child, but all that is in the background and no longer the main thing in your life.*
>
> *When you come back on leave you'll be yearning for your log cabin and will only be half here. You yourself write that if you were here you would yearn to be at the Front. You have experienced battle now and stood face-to-face with death. I always endeavored to understand your wish to go into battle. . . . But I can't take it anymore.*
>
> *An unmarried man like Hans or Dieter may write in this way, but it's not appropriate for the father of two small children and [the husband] of a wife, about whose love and loyalty you can be certain. If our marriage was childless, or we were not happy together it would be different. But given the way it is between us, it is just not acceptable.*
>
> *You should thank God that you are still alive and long for nothing more ardently than to return to those who are yours. If you were to be among the fallen now, then that would be just fine, wouldn't it? I would ask you not to proceed with any more requests to return home, which incidentally I don't believe in the least. Just act from now on as if you had no family, volunteer for the Front or the Waffen SS, so that you won't have any complexes later on when you face the local farmers here. Do what you are driven to by your devotion and duty to the Fatherland, and never mind us. Volunteer for England or whatever seems right to you. We have no desire to hold you back.*

This bitter sarcasm followed the outbursts of frustration and incandescent fury. One senses that the pent-up desolation at the mockery of her hopes by the course of the war had finally erupted and was being projected onto Ernst. It all poured out as she went on to talk about the tensions with his Sommer relatives and her disappointment that he had not supported her more strongly vis-à-vis them:

> *I have worried and prayed, wept and despaired. When the challenges you overcame seemed inhuman, my dearest wish was that*

---

76. Ernst had previously met Lilo's suspicion that he was happy as a soldier, that he enjoyed the comradeship of the army, the chances to meet attractive young women, and the availability of alcohol; cf. Ernst to Lilo, May 26, 1941.

you avoid hostile fire and stay alive. My letters to you were all actuated by concern and love. That I have gone to the dogs, physically and psychically, is the direct outcome of my concern for you. When I reread the letters I sent to you it all comes alive again. I've put away unread my letters that were returned today. Have you been able to sense anything of my distress and my desolation on your behalf? You find everything hunky dory, after all: it all seems obvious and straightforward.

I worry about you in the looming Russian winter: you look forward to riding on sledges. What's the point of me saying anything at all? All I can put down on paper is my love, yearning, and worries. I have not learnt to put aside my egoism. I am not yet ready to abandon the hope of happiness. I would like once again to be free of worry and anxieties, that's the sort of person I am. I would like to dance again, be joyful, and enjoy life.

This is now the third year in which I am on my own. I have given birth to Hartmut in your absence and brought him up without you, looked after the children's education and all their needs on my own, taken meticulous care of the house and the garden and all the rest of it. None of that was easy. Above all the children demand so much nervous energy, of which my store is not limitless. How often you've said to [your sister] Leni: 'How strained and worn out you are, the children really exhaust you.' And she had a husband at her side. Do you think it's any different for me? You only experience your children for a few days at a time, when everything seems just fine. But what you don't know about is the patience, work and long-suffering that is required year after year to bring up children.

On top of that there was the worry about you, the bombers over Wrohm and above all just staying here [in Spantekow], which completely exhausts me. I simply cannot live in this atmosphere, and want so very much to be in my own place. I don't know what's to become of us all. I'm stuck here, the bombers fly over Wrohm, and I would be without a maid there, more importantly without the company of any human being, alone, day and night. I've reason enough to be tired of the war, while you can't get enough of the fighting, and find our own life so unimportant. I see the war as a necessary evil, but my enthusiasm and my idealism have completely evaporated.

You write, what's the point of worrying about the future? Well, it's all very well for you to talk, when you are so far away from it. You'll resolve things when you come on leave? Well, it's going to be a long wait for that. Whether at Christmas or straight away. I can't answer that for you. You must know that for yourself. It'll only be a year by February since you were here last. Yes we have become hard, you at least, my own wild thoughts make it difficult for me. You have the right approach, and I should adopt it too.

I am really feeling very low and more abandoned than ever. Husband and wife will no doubt seldom be of one mind about the war. I am neither brave nor heroic and fine words mean nothing to me. You'll probably find a more understanding ear in Gerda [Hans's fiancée], although she has not been through what I have with my parents, and has no children to care for. But I have fought for and found happiness and a home at your side and found balm for my soul, which made me a cheerful, happy human being. The war robs me of all that, especially when you come to terms with it with such panache.

Our children are well. I'm sure you will be aware that it´s my love for you that is speaking in all this. I continue to wish you every happiness. Your Lilo.[77]

As another letter five days later attests, she was indeed at her wits' end, thin as a rake with worry, her nerves in tatters, sleepless because of air raids, criticized by her family in Spantekow for not disciplining her children enough (though she took the stick to both of them at times), and worried stiff about Ernst.[78] Personal distress flowed into her mounting fears about the military situation. While she did not abandon all hope of final victory, there was little but despair in her heart by the end of 1941. As she noted, something like fifty officers in his regiment had fallen already.[79]

Ernst was paralyzed with horror when he received this letter:

A storm rages all round me. I am shivering all over. I am frozen stiff, utterly horrified. That was what your letter of 12 October did to me. On top of the nervous tension brought about by the fighting we've been in nonstop since 22 June, on top of the extreme physical challenges there was always my concern for my dear ones, which never left me since the day we parted, not even in the hours when we faced the heaviest fire, nor in the quiet hours when we could enjoy some respite. Throughout the bitterest fighting I never forgot the distress of a loving wife, who had to face the possible death of her husband. It was this that forced me to say nothing about the ghastly sides to this war;

---

77. Lilo to Ernst, October 12, 1941; letters in the following two days have a more measured tone, though she suspects he would prefer to spend Christmas with his men in the blockhouse; however on October 15, 1941 she reproaches herself terribly for the bitter letter to him.
78. Lilo to Ernst, October 17, 1941.
79. Lilo to Ernst, December 5, 1941; December 10, 1941.

about the many, many dead and wounded, about the horrendous images of those who had been murdered, about feet and chunks of flesh flying over my head, about the decomposing Russian bodies in a foxhole I leaped into to escape the artillery fire, about the charcoaled corpses at the steering wheel of burnt-out trucks, about sickening images which will pursue me for the rest of my life. I forced myself to put to one side the stress I was under, the primitive living conditions, the pressures of loneliness, and my own longings, in order to spare my loved ones. I wanted to burn away death and all its terrors from your thoughts so you would not worry too much.

And now this dreadful letter. I am shaken to the core of my being. To avoid collapsing here you have to strain every nerve in your body. Many can't cope. I hope God will give me the strength to do so, but your last letter is no help at all. I am totally bemused when I read what you have written. Throughout the campaign my worry about you was stronger than for myself. Death only menaced me when I thought of my loved ones. If your loving letter of 13 October had not arrived at the same time I would just have howled in pain. In it you ask me to respond to the letter of 12 October. I cannot. I am only sad and shattered and ask myself, does Lilo really believe that I am happy and contented here? Oh this distress in my heart! If you continue to torture me like this, it will devour me. . . . You are my last support in this most ghastly of all wars. I can't take any more.[80]

When she got this letter Lilo felt absolutely dreadful:

O my dear Ernst,
  Now the letter has arrived which I have been so anxiously awaiting. It made me quite ill. You made me very ashamed and I ask your forgiveness for the wrong I have done you. But in all your recent letters I had the feeling that you lacked for nothing. And I just could not understand it, especially as I suffer so much from this war and our separation. I have never had strong nerves, having been sinned against too much as a child, and now the worries about you, the fear of the bombers, all the hassle at Wrohm, the children, and to cap it all, the atmosphere here, completely wear me down. If the war lasts another two years, I'll be finished and will need to take a cure.
  Try to understand the letter in that light and don't be so sad. I am perturbed that you suffer so much from it. I certainly don't wish to torture you, as you put it. I love you more than I can possibly say, and cannot share your attitude to the war as you expressed it in the letters. But today's letter has completely convinced me that

---

80. Ernst to Lilo, October 22, 1941.

Russia

it's different. I am now in such distress for you, how much easier it would be if you were here and could talk it through. Always this being on your own!

Dear Ernst, you know that I can take it better if you say how it is, rather than being silent about it. In the future tell me how things are, is that possible? I worry about you. At the Volkhov Front, no great distance from you, all sorts of things went on, and I fear that the air won't be clear where you are either. And since you have also left your little house, my mind has been racing. Is the field kitchen no longer nearby?

Ach yes, what lies before us? How I thank God that we are still alive, in view of all that you describe. It will take time till you can put aside all that horrible stuff. I really think I will be in awe of you, when I have you back again, so much lies between us, you have experienced too much. It is so long, too, since we were together. If only the tension could finally be dispelled and calmed and our hearts could relax again. You once wrote of the blessing of war, my Ernst, I curse it, it brings suffering and death. May God continue to grant you his protection and the nerves to bear it all. I won't cause you any more worry. I am really so sorry. Every day the paper reports more men fallen. This SU the Russians talk of means Soviet Union. The guys look like phantoms, completely drained. They can hardly walk. They gobble grass, potatoes, turnips, as they are starving here, too. This crazy war, it is nothing but murder. Tell me what you think, some time, won't you, please? I keep looking at the images.

A parcel goes off tomorrow again. Your cigarettes arrived. Are you not smoking any more? The choco[late] was wonderful, but please, please keep it for yourself! I imagine the photos will please you. Your 'wee lad' is pure gold, eh? He'll be sure to warm your heart. I only live for you, dear Ernst, and want so much to be good for you, especially since I have saddened you. Get well again, and keep on cherishing me.

For ever, your Lilo.[81]

The directness, the emotional nakedness, the acerbity of this interchange is the flip side to the quality of their relationship. As the reference to the Volkhov Front shows, Lilo had kept herself informed about what was to develop in the coming months into a ferocious battle, as the Russian army sought to relieve the siege of Leningrad and halt the advance on Moscow. The way the war was developing had put impossible demands on their commitment to each other. In its veracity and directness, this part of

---

81. Lilo to Ernst, November 1, 1941.

the correspondence is truly remarkable. Both Lilo and Ernst strove to speak truth to one another, to maintain and nourish their love for one another as their worlds disintegrated around them. On this occasion, as so often before, they made their peace with one another. She was soon "his old Lilo" again. Yet of course things had been said that could not be forgotten. How much raw pain could their relationship absorb and transcend?

Frost, ice, and snow were now the order of the day for him. He had to leave the block house, as the Front moved forwards, and though his new peasant home was warm enough Ernst became sharply aware of the need for more winter clothing. He also had to struggle with lice, fleas, and bedbugs; no amount of washing, brushing, and changing his underclothes would dispel them. Morning and evening he and his companions stripped off and went to war on their tormentors. Candles had run out, too, and by 3 p.m. it was pitch black.[82] The few, amateurish photos that survive illustrate vividly how intolerable the conditions were becoming for the battalion. They are of course amply documented from countless other sources.

In this pre-Christmas period, though, there were virtually no hostilities on their section of the Front. Unknown to them the Russian forces were busily regrouping, biding their time. Ernst's men passed the days as best they could, ate and slept, played board games, including a chess set they had improvised, listened to records on a confiscated Russian gramophone, played the mouth organ, went for walks, wrote letters, read, and thought about home.[83]

One welcome change in the daily monotony was a visit to the sauna in a neighboring village. It was a primitive affair. Large stones had been hauled in from the fields and a large fire lit around them. Once the smoke was dispelled, eight men crept into the room, bent almost double. Buckets of cold water were then thrown onto the stones, and the room filled with steam. They began to sweat mightily, and the hot, damp air cleared out the chest. Their lousy clothes were hung up high and by the time the sauna was finished, twenty minutes or so later, they were once again bone dry. A bucket of cold water thrown over them by the *Bademeister* (the bath attendant)

---

82. Ernst to Lilo, October 29, 1941; November 2, 1941; November 5, 1941.

83. "Of late our gramophone has been the real highlight for us. We exchange records, and lap up the music, both the Russian and German songs; among the German ones are 'I have a little mandolin'; 'Can you hear *mein heimliches Rufen* (my hidden cry)?'; 'Do come home, I'm so longing for you, *all mein Glück* (my only joy)'; Lilo, do you know that one?" Ernst to Lilo, November 10, 1941.

ended the process. The sauna tired you out, and whetted the appetite, but it was healthy, refreshing, and above all, it "spells death to the lice."[84]

In mid-November Lilo wrote Ernst a touching love letter. She was already thinking ahead to Christmas. Amid the carnage of the war and the incessant hammering of the Party propaganda she had her own inner calendar, so to speak; it was a domestic one, and a Christian one. She navigated her way from one birthday or family anniversary to the next, from Easter to Whitsun or Christmas. War might be omnipresent, but it was not totalitarian, all-encompassing; it did not wholly determine the rhythm of her life:

> *By the time you get this letter, dearest, there will only be four weeks at most to Christmas. Last year when I sat on my own in Wrohm, I comforted myself with the thought that it would all pass, next year everything would be good again, better than ever. I had a footing, though, in the happy world of my own home and felt geborgen (at peace) as a result. . . . My dear little children are what give me strength now, I know who I am when I stand beside their beds at night, and when I look at their sleeping faces I am once again the old loving Lilo. I feel the warmth of [my daughter's] little body, Hartmut's fresh, clean breath. They are your flesh and blood, my dearest man. You provided the foundation for their life.*
>
> *And yet the children are not enough for me; again and again I look towards you and towards life at your side. I would like to reach up higher, to extend myself, to grow inwardly until I become more and more like you. You have often said that your love is both challenge and support to me. I now know what I would lack if you were not there. And the crowning glory is that you, too, need me, and are happy to receive my love. I am hungry for you and have an unspeakable longing for you. In such unending love I remain your wee lass, Deine Deern, Lilo.*

Her imagination painted in glowing colors his return on leave from the privations of the Front to the comforts of home, his delight in the children, and their own personal reunion.[85] Ernst was hugely touched by this letter. It spoke to him of home, of love, of paradise on earth, and gave him the strength to endure.[86] Lilo's letter of December 2 again reflects her awareness of the Russian counteroffensives from the end of October, when

---

84. Ernst to Lilo, November 8, 1941.
85. Lilo to Ernst, November 15, 1941; November 20, 1941.
86. Ernst to Lilo, December 3, 1941.

the Germans were driven back after initially taking Rostov. Her brother, Dieter, had also alerted her to Russian artillery fire near Ernst's position, much to Ernst's annoyance, who assured Lilo they were entirely safe in their bunker.

My dear Ernst, my tension eased off a bit today as lots of loving mail arrived from you, from the 18th, 20th, 22nd, and the 23rd of November. Thank you, my Ernst. But as you know the 26th is the key day, and so my worries remain the same. The next days may bring me relief, when I know, hopefully, that you have got through it all well. These encroachments by the Reds will continue. I read about 24 October with astonishment. [Unclear what is referred to here.] You had never mentioned this in your letters.

You dear man, you only write about the restful times. But now I know that they are only momentary. The Russian must still feel strong, otherwise he wouldn't be doing what he does. My dearest, let's accept that once again we won't be together for Christmas. I am preparing myself for the thought that there will be no leave until the spring or even the summer. The rail connections will not improve; rather deteriorate as more ground is won. There will be no leave until everything is over in Russia. And when will that be? There will be no end ever and from the Caucasus it will go on to Suez etc. The goal is ambitious and no end is in sight. Herr Graming talked yesterday evening of his four winters in Russia. He didn't get leave for a year and three-quarters.

Christmas won't be easy for us, Darling. But I will thank God if you are still alive. How dreadful the celebrations must be for those who have lost their beloved! How you will be yearning for the children. If I as their mother were away from my children so much it would make me ill. Heinke prays so touchingly: 'Dear, good Father Christmas. Don't look angrily at me. Put away your stick. I'll always be good.' Father Christmas must appear in person. Let's see if Herr Stack will do it. And Heinke sings the carols: "O Tannenbaum" ("O Christmas Tree") and "Alle Jahre wieder" ("Once More Each Year"). As darkness falls she always begs me: "Mutti, tell a story." And our wee toddler comes along too, although he doesn't understand much, but is quiet as a mouse and listens. Hartmut is such a dear boy. He throws a hand kiss to Russia for Pappi.

Today when we were baking Pfeffernüsse (gingernuts), Heinke was a great help. She rolled up her sleeves and then rolled the nuts between her palms. When a tray of gingernuts came out of the oven she said: 'Oh, how wonderful!!' She already speaks of 'my mother, my father.' Yes, Pappi, you will be astonished at your big little girl. It'll be quite strange for you when you see your big children again.

Marvelous that my parcels have already arrived. I thought they should be there for Advent. How wonderful that you are so pleased! But you've guessed wrong about the present. I'll give you another tip. It's in four parts, so have another guess!

Darling, what does 'old comrades' mean?[87] Has one to have been in action in France and Poland already? It seems to me that Russia trumps everything, and the key question is who wasn't at home last year, and who has children. All this about medals doesn't seem right to me.

My Ernst, I couldn't get cough tablets. They don't make them anymore because of the sugar shortage.... Aren't the winter clothes there yet? God grant that you are well, dearest. I long to hear. Your Lilofrau upholds you in prayer and in her fiery love. Warm greetings from the parents. Full moon today, which always makes me bomber-crazy.[88]

Another moving love letter was written by Lilo for Ernst to read on Christmas Eve. In it she reaffirmed that she was his, body, mind, and soul. Their love soared above all that separated them. He would not be alone; her love would encompass him, his homeland would be close at hand. She imagined him unpacking her presents, that little red lantern she has sent him, then reading her letters, and singing the beloved German carols. When he lay down on his hard bed to rest, he should imagine her arms around his neck, her head on his breast, and go to sleep in her embrace. "What a glorious, pure, and profound love ours is." She thanked him for all the good things he had bestowed on her, for his faith in her goodness. Her life belonged to him, and it would be devoted to the children in whom his blood flowed so strongly.[89] Reading this letter, Ernst wrote back, was like lying on the couch, his head on her lap, her hands caressing him.[90]

He imagines making a surprise visit home, listening to the beating of her heart as he lay in her arms. Again and again he talked of the blessing of their relationship, what he again called a river, a torrent of love, as in his letter to his "dearly beloved Lilo" on New Year's Day 1940. Writing from the Russian Front in December 1941 he imagined sleeping at her breast,

87. The term refers to those who had joined the National Socialist German Workers' Party before 1930; they had priority for leave.
88. Lilo to Ernst, December 2, 1941.
89. Lilo to Ernst, December 12, 1941.
90. Ernst to Lilo, December 24, 1941.

enjoying the stillness, forgetting everything that was ugly and mean, just savoring her love. His tears would flow. "I so long for you, for your blond hair, your dear eyes, your kisses, your marvelous body, everything, everything."[91] All this just two months before his death.

---

91. *. . . wie gern würde ich mich von meinem Frauchen verwöhnen lassen, an Deiner Brust schlafen und ganz stille werden in Deiner Liebe und alles, alles Häßliche vergessen. Ich glaube, mir würden vor Glück die Tränen kommen. Ich sehne mich ja so unendlich nach dir, dein blondes Haar, Deine lieben Augen, Dein Küssen, Dein wunderbarer Körper, alles, alles.* Ernst to Lilo, December 3, 1941.

5

The Last Days

Human beings suffer
They torture one another,
They get hurt and get hard.
—SEAMUS HEANEY, 1990

CHRISTMAS EVE 1941 HAD brought Lilo little joy, except vicariously through the excitement of the children, but she wrote Ernst a brave and positive letter on Christmas Day. It described a brief visit to the church in Spantekow, going up with little Heinke to the organ gallery to see her father playing; then she pictured the anticipation and excitement of the children when they got home, the candlelit Christmas tree, and the mountain of presents for the children, the high points being a large homemade wooden train, and a talking doll in a pram for Heinke. All this made Lilo aware that she was supported by a host of family and friends. She was not alone. There were picture books galore for the children and books for herself. A huge basket of flowers from her brother, Dieter, brought tears to her eyes.

Her thoughts turned, of course, to Ernst in the awful cold and amid the ferocity of the fighting. She focused in her letter, though, on their hopes for the future, and on the delight of the children in the singing of the carols. "Good night, dear Ernst, I hope all goes well, may God preserve you."[1] The

---

1. Lilo to Ernst, February 26, 1941.

words to him the previous month would have been particularly apposite at Christmas: "Every night I sleep at your heart."[2]

Ernst, in turn, wrote her a touching, atmospheric letter on Christmas Eve:

> *My dearest, my thoughts sweep towards you away out over the dark, gloomy woods, the burned-out villages, the endless steppes of Russia, out over the cold splendor of Winter. . . . This infinitude of whiteness is like a shroud. It lies gently and compassionately on the blood-soaked earth as if to lessen the agony of recent events. . . .*
>
> *And yet, the German soldier lives. His longing heart preserves him from despair. The hope of better days springs up like a green shoot; his yearning for this is mirrored in the German Christmas tree. Every foxhole has its little tree. . . . And they will shine out in the dark night from the Arctic to the Black Sea. Our hearts will be at peace and our souls will wander homewards. They will be quiet and as they wander homewards their faith in the light will be strong. The good will triumph . . . I will let myself be caught up in God's love and grace. I will be found by the Christ child and my heart will rejoice in Christmas hope.*
>
> *Dearest, let us believe in God's love and in his almighty power, joyfully accept the Christmas message and foster the hope that everything will change for the better. Our love joins us together and gives us the power to believe, to hope, to remain true. A Christmas angel will carry me gently to you. From my heart I greet you, my dearest Lilo and you, you dear little children.*
>
> *Your Papa.*[3]

His comrades reported that he talked to Lilo in his sleep; he was aware that he often dreamt of her. He would just shut his eyes and imagine the children playing, and wonder what songs they were singing.[4] He was quite aware, though, of how much work the children were for Lilo. As 1942 began he rejoiced that their love for one another was as strong and fiery as ever; it was such a delight, too, to hear how much Heinke loved singing. "The more the Russians attack us over ice and snow the better. The loss of blood will be dramatic and ease the way for the German forces in the summer."[5] One

---

2. Lilo to Ernst, November 30, 1941.
3. Ernst to Lilo, December 24, 1941.
4. Ernst to Lilo, December 20, 1941; December 31, 1941.
5. Ernst to Lilo, January 3, 1942.

The Last Days

senses his mind jumping from one thing to the next, from Spantekow to the Russian Front, from children to hostile attacks, from one world to the next.

New Year's Eve felt ominous and heavy for Lilo, with Wagner's *Götterdämmerung* ringing in her ears from the radio, and the "earnestness" of the Führer's speech weighing on her. She recalled that Ernst's views on the course of the war had been too optimistic from the very beginning; the opposite had turned out to be the case. She felt, too, that if he had been less obliging to others he would have got leave by now. For the first time she considered the grave consequences if Germany were to lose the war, while quickly reassuring herself that a final victory was of course certain. The thought of all the German blood that would flow in the East was again uppermost in her mind.[6] Occasionally Ernst had hinted at the likelihood of leave in his letters, but it had never come to anything.[7]

Then in a more lyrical letter she responded to Ernst's description of Christmas at the Front, which had brought tears to her eyes:

> *What an occasion it will be when we are together again. I know my young man, his beating heart and the vigor of his love. You once said to me that a real man must have vitality. For me there is nothing more wonderful than to abandon myself to you, the one and only person who has ever, and who will ever in the future, make me his own.* [Her sole desire was for him, the man who kept returning to her in her dreams, though sometimes she was baffled by a strange expression on his face. Reality and dream were playing tricks on them both. Every day she must be prepared to give him up for the sake of the Fatherland. That, however, she could not do. Her only wish in that case would be to follow him into death. But of course she could not do that to their children.] *I would have to live on with a bleeding heart. It would be pure torture and never-diminishing pain. We all have to bear what God has determined for us.*[8]

A grim prediction of what in fact lay ahead of her.

When her letters of January 11 and then others were returned as undeliverable she was alarmed beyond words, terrified that her worst fears were about to be realized, although she was aware of rumors of a *Postsperre* (a temporary suspension of the postal service). The suffering caused by the war was like a dead weight on her. There was no joy to life anymore. "*Mir ist das Leben so über* (I'm so over it)," she would write. She saw quite

---

6. Lilo to Ernst, January 2, 1942.
7. Ernst to Lilo, November 6, 1941.
8. Lilo to Ernst, January 6, 1942.

realistically that the war in the East would drag on, that Britain would retaliate, and even predicted that American bombs would soon be raining down on Germany.[9] On January 23 she lamented that it had been three weeks since she last heard from him. By January 31 there was still no mail. Not a single letter had come from him in January.

To add to her despair, her mother's treatment of her was becoming intolerable. She thought of returning to Wrohm but knew that it would be going to rack and ruin in the damp and the cold. The newspapers were full of reports of fierce fighting around the Ilmensee, where Ernst was. She pictured this and the ferocious cold, up to thirty-eight degrees below. Her heart plummeted to the very depths as she imagined Ernst trying to cope with this. It was utterly inhuman that he had been on the front line nonstop, and never relieved.[10] She could not stop the flow of tears when she envisaged him battling such conditions. In fact a card from Ernst on January 20 spoke of incredible, fierce cold, forty-two degrees below. His mind, though, was already beginning to focus on his daughter's birthday on February 12.

It is clear that Ernst became involved in heavy fighting once again as soon as the new year began. A letter of his to another soldier, his friend Willi Falkemeier, gave an unvarnished account of the conditions. "The fighting is fierce here. We had been virtually abandoned near Staraja Russa, but then secured some air support.... We are now lying in our bunkers face-to-face with the Russians.... Anti-tank guns, mortars, machine guns bang away every day...." He was full of praise for his men, mostly north Germans. There had been a massive attack by the Russians way back in October, and the hundred and fifty enemy corpses still lay in front of their minefield, covered by the snow. He had been away from wife and family now for three years, who were longing to see him, but leave, he complained, seemed to be a matter of luck, a complete lottery.[11]

Lilo's letter of February 10 contained a vivid account of the children singing as they slid down on the sledge, and of them shoveling away the snow. Heinke was looking forward eagerly to her third birthday on the twelfth. Written to Ernst the day before his death, this letter was never received.[12]

9. Lilo to Ernst, January 11, 1942.
10. Lilo to Ernst, January 25, 1942.
11. Ernst to Willi Falkemeier, January 5, 1942.
12. *Muschi träumt ihrem "Burtstag" entgegen und singt, "Ich freue mich, daß ich geboren bin und hab Geburtstag heut."* Lilo to Ernst, December 10, 1941.

The Last Days

There is a bitter irony about Lilo's next letter, reporting tiredly but enthusiastically about Heinke's birthday, and recalling Ernst's closeness to her through the ordeal of the birth. As the wild snowstorm howled around Spantekow, she thought of the likelihood that the Russians would be using such storms as cover for an attack. She implored God's protection for him. But he was already dead as she put pen to paper.[13]

It is ghoulish, somehow, to read the letters she continued to send off. And then, still worse: she began, still not knowing that he was in fact dead, to receive letters he had sent off in his last days of life. On the third of February he had written that he found the stoppage of mail cruel, but hoped that she enough letters had got through to reassure her that he was well. He was living in a warm peasant house. The Russians baked rye bread for them, and now and then cooked a chicken, but "staying in this accursed land has the soul always on the edge of a precipice," especially with the lack of mail and the prohibition that was now in force on even discussing leave. Only the memories of home and the comradeship of his fellow soldiers kept him going. His thoughts were always with her; it was like a fairy tale to think of being with one's own children again. Here one only saw ragged Russian children. Lilo and he had not seen one another now for nearly a year. It was incredible what one could endure, but each day was a struggle to keep alert. "May the Lord God grant me strength."[14]

A card sent off from him on February 6, confirming the receipt of her loving letters of January 2 and 14 convinced her that all was well; and she sent him a kiss. Another card of his from 9 February enthused about the snapshots of the children; they were just wonderful.

In a letter on February 22 she described a wonderful ride through the snow, the bells on the sledge tinkling away merrily. Neighbors had taken her and Heinke on a long trip through the sunlit countryside, the deep snow often being up to the horses' bellies. In the evening she had switched on the radio, and imagined dancing in his arms to the music, like the young woman she once was.[15] Other letters written at this time reveal that she

---

13. Lilo to Ernst, February 12, 1942; the weather condition were appalling; General Heinrici: "The wind stabs you in the face with needles, and blasts through your protective headgear and your gloves. Your eyes are streaming so much that you can hardly see a thing." There were huge problems with frostbite and grossly inadequate clothing and equipment, compared with the Soviet ski battalions and light cavalry. Hürter, *Ein Deutscher General*, 108, quoted Evans, *The Third Reich at War*, 207.

14. Ernst to Lilo, February 3, 1942.

15. Lilo to Ernst, February 18, 1942; February 22, 1942.

was aware of the heavy Russian artillery fire around Staraja Russa. Letters of other soldiers on the Russian Front, describing the ferocity of the attacks, had come into her hands. She was mystified by this robust Russian resistance and by the many warplanes they could deploy. A lovingly packed parcel of goodies, including chocolate, cakes, and marmalade did not get through to him, to her huge disappointment.

Incomparably worse, she had the agonizing task of composing a letter to inform her (dead) husband of the death of his younger brother, Hans. No letter had ever been more difficult to write:

> *My dear, dear man. This letter is impossibly difficult for me. I can find no words to express which is troubling me and making me so endlessly sad. Your beloved Hans-brother! What a terrible blow it must be to you, dear man, shaking you to the very core. [Ernst and Hans had been so close, she knew. His pain was her pain. She thought of their mother, a widow from the First World War, whose faith had been unshakeable that her two boys still had tasks to fulfill and that they would win through; and of the unspeakable sadness of his wife, Gerda, now a young widow.]*[16]

She also assured her mother-in-law that their house would always be open to her, that she would be sure to find a home with her and Ernst.

Ernst's mother, on hearing of the death of Hans, had at once written to the army authorities asking for immediate leave for Ernst, in the light of his bereavement, but Lilo believed that the chances for that were poor. She worried about her own brother, Dieter, who had been wounded several times but was back in the thick of it, his division in disarray, patched up with troops from other divisions.[17]

> *My beloved husband!*
>
> *My thoughts are with you nonstop, with you alone. I can't think about anything else except how you are doing, and how the telegram about Hans's death has affected you. On top of everything else you've*

---

16. *Unser Hartmut, Dein Ebenbild, trägt auch dein Leben weiter. Gäbe ein gnädiger Gott Dich uns und Deiner Mutter zurück, er schütze und behüte Dich und gebe die Kraft an Leib und Seele, alles zu ertragen. Ich bin im Leid noch enger mit Dir verbunden, Dein Schmerz ist auch mein Schmerz.* Lilo to Ernst, February 28, 1942.

17. Her brother Dieter's death was on 28 October 1943. The commander of his Regiment wrote an unusually full and thoughtful letter to his parents, stressing his exceptional courage and leadership qualities and recommending he be promoted posthumously to *Hauptmann* (captain). Kahler to Herr Struck, October 30, 1943.

The Last Days

been caught up in heavy fighting for days, demanding your total concentration. My dear, dear Ernst!

Mother wrote me to say she had sent off a telegram to you. I had feared she would. A telegram like that is so heartless; its curt, ominous message devastates one. But Mother desperately wants you to be with her to help her get on her feet again. You must come, Ernst, please see the colonel about it. Mother has sent off a request for leave, though I am not at all hopeful. By the time the request has gone through one official instance after another and reaches you weeks will have passed; and then whether or not it will be approved is another matter altogether. So many officers are here for more training and leave again on the 15th for the Front. So one could make an exception in your case and let you join your mother after you've been there a whole year without leave.

But times are so hard and merciless. We keep hearing about heavy, unremitting fighting to the southeast of Lake Il'men. What a ghastly war this is! Never before have there been so many death notices in the papers, almost daily, 7, 6, 4 of them, whether in the Heide or the Anklam paper. Whole columns of them in the Völkischer Beobachter! What losses we have to bear, fatalities, men frozen to death. All the field hospitals crammed full. Oh, this war, what human beings have to suffer, and what is being achieved by it all? Even here in the village fate has its way with us, as soon as one piece of bad news is digested, another is there. It's enough to scare you stiff. I lie in bed, unable to sleep, thinking of Hans, of Gerda, of you out there. Ach, my Ernst, stay safe! I am really struggling; all peace of mind is gone.

Dieter, too, appears to be encircled with the company he is commanding. His division has been badly mauled and its communications are in disarray. For the moment he belongs to the 269th Division, which was mentioned recently in the news. His position is on the Luga, south of Leningrad and northwest of Novgorod. We have lost quite a bit of ground.

Yesterday I sent off a parcel for you with Schwarzkopf, who also got a hunk of sausage. If only it reaches you, which I rather doubt. There are three or four letters from me with it. Have you had any of my letters since that of 17 December? I've now been seven weeks without getting any sign of life from you. Just now, at the beginning of March your letters of 6 and 7 January arrived. Is the postal stoppage over at last? I gathered that from your letter. If only I had a photo of you. Did you get our snaps? If all your letters arrive at once, there'll be a whole sacksful for you. Tomorrow is Hans's birthday!

Oh, Ernst, what a mournful business, come back to us for goodness sake. I am yours and think of you in deep, inward unity. Your Lilo.[18]

As a letter on March 11, a full month after Ernst's death, testifies, she still clung onto the hope that Ernst might be alive, but his last letter had been written five weeks before, and as more of her letters came back as undeliverable, she could not stem the flow of tears. It was her wedding anniversary, the day before her little boy's second birthday. She wondered if Ernst was in a casualty station. "I've never been so overwhelmed with anxiety and worry."[19]

He was long dead, in fact, hastily buried with other comrades beside the railway line near Borki, on the stretch between Borki and Owscha, some twenty-five kilometers from the city of Staraja Russa. After the war Ernst's grave could no longer be identified. The official notification of his death by Major Geerkens had been written, punctually enough, on February 16, but took an eternity to reach her, having been mistakenly sent to the Wrohm address. When she eventually received it she authorized the following death announcement in the paper:

> *On my wedding anniversary I received the devastating news, that on 11.2.41, the birthday of his little daughter, my dearly beloved husband, the joyous father of his little children, the caring eldest son of his mother, the leader of the 3/85 section of the Hitler Youth, the teacher Ernst Sommer, Lieutenant of [his] Infantry Regiment, bearer of the Iron Cross (second class), crowned his life for family, Führer, Nation and Fatherland with a heroic death in a fierce battle with Bolshevism. He followed his father, who had died in the World War, and his only brother, who perished on the Crimean peninsula. His affirmation: 'An infinitely happy marriage is my strength' is my own light and my support.*
>
> *In limitless gratitude, love and loyalty.*
>
> *Liselotte Sommer, née Struck, Heinke and Hartmut. Spantekow. Wrohm, Dithmarschen War Heroes Day, 1942.*[20]

---

18. Lilo to Ernst, March 3, 1942.

19. Lilo to Ernst, February 25, 1942; February 27, 1942; February 28, 1942; March 1, 1942; March 3, 1942; March 6, 1942; March 11, 1942.

20. The death notice she authorized was in conventional language; she had nothing else at her disposal. It appeared on 21 March, the *Heldengedenktag* (Memorial Day), when pompous ceremonies in Berlin and elsewhere celebrated the heroic deaths of those who had fallen for the Fatherland. Shortly afterwards she received the Demjansk shield, commissioned by Hitler to commemorate the troops who fell there; the language of Ernst's mother, who within four weeks had lost both her sons, Ernst and Hans, in her

The Last Days

In the extremity of her grief she had resorted to the conventional language of the Third Reich about a heroic death for the Fatherland. What else did she have at her disposal? The children were cared for by relatives as she collapsed. She went to Berlin for a while, to Gerda, Hans's widow. One is struck by the fortitude of her letters to others, including to Ernst's mother, who was now doubly bereaved. They were remarkably brave and outgoing.

Letters from his comrades at the Front spoke of Ernst with affection, distress, and real sympathy for Lilo, his wife. This war had been unrelenting. His had been a heroic death for the Fatherland, and he had remained true to his sacred soldierly oath as a German officer. Lilo herself had written in her Christmas letter to him: "You are Adolf Hitler's true soldier, prepared to offer up your life for Germany and the future of our children."[21]

According to Corporal Amst, they had launched an assault on February 10, 1942, which went well, but were unable to dislodge the enemy. On the morning of February 11 Lieutenant Sommer was then hit in the stomach just in front of the trench. His last words were; "Greet my wife and children; my daughter is 3 years old today." He died in peace but the enemy advanced in overwhelming force, and all Amst could take with him was the lieutenant's pay book and map case. Other comrades had buried him. The lieutenant had been a shining example of heroic courage to all of them.[22]

"Such sacrifices," wrote his close friend, the officer Karl Magerhans, lying wounded in a field hospital, and soon to be among the fallen himself, "are necessary . . . but will never be in vain. It is my unshakeable conviction that in this coming year the good Lord will bless our weapons with success." It was unbearably painful for him to write to her about the heroic death of her beloved husband, their dear and respected comrade. Till his last breath he had been the inspiration of his men, and had died rifle in hand, defending his field gun against the overwhelming forces of the Russians.[23]

His fellow officers and NCOs obviously portrayed the circumstances of his death in as positive a light as possible for his widow, but there seems

---

acknowledgement of the sympathy she had received is similar, their *Heldentod* (heroic death), giving their life to the Fatherland.

21. Lilo to Ernst, December 12, 1941.

22. Corporal Amst to Lilo, April 5, 1942; he apologized for the delay in writing; clearly Lilo had asked for more information about Ernst's death; given the rapid retreat, it is improbable that his comrades buried him; the local Russians may have buried him beside the railway line.

23. Karl Magerhans to Lilo, March 1, 1942; note the absence of National Socialist rhetoric and of *Heil Hitler*.

no reason to doubt the substance of their reports. Something of their own humanity and vulnerability shines through, though if anything it only enhances the barbarism of the whole campaign.

The same can be said of the quality of the relationship between Ernst and Lilo. One suspects that few officers or men, and few of the wives and lovers left at home, would have been sustained by such an authentic meeting of minds and hearts as we see in this correspondence. Together they had faced the prospect of his imminent death long before it actually took place. We cannot begin to reconstruct what both of them went through in these last days, but there is a sense in which they were prepared for the worst.

The official history notes that the encircled Germans were vastly outnumbered. The significance of Borki was that its defense kept the route for supplies open, and enabled the encirclement of the German troops to be broken.[24] The children at Lilo's father's school at Spantekow listened with hands folded in prayer to the tolling of the church bell and sang the sentimental song "Ich hatt' einen Kameraden" ("I Had a Comrade"), and thought of Lilo's "dear little children." The teacher signed off with a *Heil Hitler*.[25] There were also floods of cards and letters from neighbors, friends, and family. Lilo kept them all. It is impossible to read them without realizing in a new and stark way the cost of National Socialism's nihilism to ordinary German people. They are human and personal, precisely the qualities being jettisoned by the Nazi leadership. The easy words about a heroic death for the Fatherland are few and far between.

Ernst seems to have had a premonition of his coming death. Magerhans wrote on March 2:

> *I've just heard some details from a comrade, to judge by which Ernst had a premonition. On the previous day he said by the river Pola to one of the sergeants: 'If I do not come back, greet my dear wife and the children. And if it has to be, then I am glad to die for the Fatherland.' One thing is sure. In his thoughts he was so very often with his dear ones back home. When we met for the last time, I had the impression that he was absentminded and scarcely listening to*

---

24. A new song was born: *Wir kamen von Norden gezogen / und sprengten bei Borki den Ring. / Die Riegel sind aufgeflogen, die Schlinge gelöst, die uns fing* (We came from the North / and burst through the ring at Borki. / The bolt has been pushed back, / the noose shaken off which throttled us); Bauer, *290. Infanterie Division. Weg und Schicksal*, 202.

25. The teacher and children from the school in Spantekow to Frau Sommer (Lilo), March 14, 1942.

The Last Days

the conversation. We often spoke about leave, which was a hot topic for a while. His most fervent wish was to be back with his family as soon as possible. Iron discipline held him back. It certainly was not the intention of his superior to exploit a willing and conscientious officer. The whole situation was already so uncertain that it forced the high command to issue commands that exacted the greatest sacrifices from the individual. Shortly before my injury I took a photo of the grave. I will send it to you as soon as possible. Borki lies on the Pola, about 50 km southeast of Staraja Russa.[26]

There is a sense in which Lilo's suffering, and that of her children, only began with Ernst's death. She never remarried. All she had of him, the letters, went with her wherever she went. His sword and fiddle were treasured and safeguarded. His photo, with a candle lit below it on special occasions, was on display. His absence was always present.

---

26. Karl Magerhans to Lilo, March 2, 1942; he had frequently stated before the war that he had no fear of dying but would much prefer a quick death on the Front to a lingering one at home. If it happened, she should not go into mourning but focus on her role as mother of their children; Ernst to Lilo, January 25, 1936.

6

The Special Significance of the Letters

Letter writing has special significance for me:
It enables me, above all, to connect with home, with you, with those closest to me, with our world as a whole;
It is my only chance to write at all;
It is my only chance to articulate who I am;
It is only as I write that much becomes evident to me;
It is my only way of keeping in touch with you and with our world.

—VACLAV HAVEL,
WRITING TO HIS WIFE FROM PRISON, 1988

How are we to read these precious letters? One writes letters because direct communication with one's partner, colleague, and friend is not available. One is no longer face-to-face. One cannot touch, hug, make love, share a meal, work together in the garden, sing or dance together, or breathe the same air.

There is always something second-best and derivative about a letter. They convey information. They can be catalysts to real communication. But for lovers, letters are emergency channels; at best they offer ersatz expression for shared delight and despair and for the resolution of differences. At times of crisis they are a necessary, but never an adequate lifeline.[1]

---

1. Esther Milne discusses the construction of imaginary presence in letters; the

The Special Significance of the Letters

Few people, moreover, have the gift of good letter writing, one which can transport the reader into the writer's habitat, and offer a glimpse into the inner world of heart and mind. Few individuals, and still fewer couples, rise to the challenge of having to keep "in touch" regularly by means of pen and ink. One needs considerable resources of time, for one thing, or the determination to make time even when tired or depressed or distracted by immediacies.[2] A strong will is a precondition to any successful correspondence.

Lilo and Ernst wrote each other assiduously despite their frequent exhaustion, and the letters are both rich in detail and remarkably frank and open. Lilo talks about menstruation, (using the code name Aunty) for example, Ernst about masturbation. In the summer of 1941 Lilo described how she had to take to bed with a high fever, which she combatted with hot milk, gargling, and grog (!).[3] Ernst could speak openly about his depressions, his tears, and his overflowing love for his children.

Above all a good letter requires imagination. People who relate well enough on a day-to-day level often fail when it comes to keeping "in touch," as we say, by writing. There are multiple reasons for this. They may have limited skills not only in self-expression, but also in articulating differences and negotiating conflicts. Ernst and Lilo, fortunately, were emotionally intelligent to an unusual degree, and on the whole found the right words to reach one another. Both were strong personalities, and told it as it was. Both could cope with criticism. Who called the shots in their marriage is not immediately obvious, though Lilo appears on the surface to be more deferential.[4] They quarreled and argued, and made up again. Their letters reflect this willingness to face and resolve conflict.

The German middle classes had a strong tradition of letter writing, and Ernst and Lilo Sommer were particularly gifted correspondents.[5] They offer little in-depth analysis of events, though, nothing remotely comparable to a Victor Klemperer or a Dietrich Bonhoeffer. Their perspectives are

---

dimensions of disembodiment, intimacy, spontaneity, and immediacy; Milne, *Letters, Postcards, Email*.

2. Responding to a criticism that his letter had been "meager," Ernst reminded Lilo that he often fell into bed exhausted at the end of a rigorous day of marching or riding. Ernst to Lilo, February 22, 1940.

3. Lilo to Ernst, June 8, 1941.

4. Lilo to Ernst, September 7, 1941; Lilo reflects on this.

5. As this is written (in 2018) surviving relatives testify that the Sommers were known as good letter writers.

largely predictable. But that is precisely the value of their correspondence. It mirrors the tragic confusion of ordinary people caught up in extraordinary events.

Ernst noted the similarity between his letters to Lilo and the diary he used to keep, which recorded his emotional highs and lows. Now he expressed these profoundly personal feelings through the letters.[6] They both observed closely their inner world and their current situation; they trusted one another with their inmost thoughts, hopes, and fears. There was no internal censor, no "scissors in the head," though their commitment to National Socialism, especially in Ernst's case, does set some boundaries to spontaneity. On political or military matters he tended to toe the Party line.

Both were able to think their way into the life and mind of the other. The separation they endured stimulated their imagination. They were determined that their love letters would bridge their unimaginably different worlds. The fierce summer heat in 1941 made Lilo aware of what Ernst was facing: the dust, sweat and exhaustion of his forced marches; and then came the wet autumn, with the mud and impassable roads for the troops in Russia, not to mention the snow and ice in a devastating winter. Ernst's letters are alert, for their part, to the endless and tedious demands on Lilo of house, garden, and children. He writes thoughtfully about the host of issues she had to cope with—from practical matters in the house or the garden to the children's health and conduct to family relationships and to her loneliness. Quite rightly they complimented one another often on how well they "painted" events.[7]

They offer us, then, vivid snapshots of reality, seen through the particular lens of their particular situation. As one reads their letters, one can smell the garden, hear the children playing, listen in to the small talk of the soldiers on the Front, sense their reception of Goebbels's propaganda and the Führer's speeches, and get a feel for Ernst's stoical courage and Lilo's growing disillusionment. "I've completely lost faith," wrote Lilo in late autumn 1941, as she saw how the Russian campaign dragged on, the RAF's bombs hailed down, and America became increasingly involved.[8]

6. Ernst to Lilo, July 26, 1940. *Mein Liebling! Früher schrieb ich ins Tagebuch, wenn seelische Hoch-oder Tiefzeiten eintrafen. Heute bist Du, mein Deern, mein Begleiter, der Freud und Leid mit mir teilt*; Edward Timms's reservations about women's letters being less frank out of fear of censorship or out of fear of seeming unpatriotic are not relevant in respect of Lilo's letters to the Front; Timms, *Anna Haag and Her Secret Diary*, 133.

7. Ernst to Lilo, June 6, 1941.

8. Lilo to Ernst, September 11, 1941.

The Special Significance of the Letters

Germany was like a "sold out" shop, she wrote on several occasions, out of everything: of shoes, clothes, and cigarettes....

To our ears these are very confused letters, more passionate than discriminating. Domestic life and patriotism, chauvinism and erotic love mingled unselfconsciously in their correspondence in a way quite foreign to us today. From one sentence to the next the letters change gear from politics or military triumphs such as the capture of Paris to delight at the progress of the toddler and baby. We know the outer landscape of the Second World War fairly accurately by now. But the "inscape" remains much more of a mystery. It is a challenge to do justice to the assuredness, the "innocence," the blinkeredness, and the rootedness of this couple.

We filter reality differently today. We who whip off a plethora of emails each day may have lost the feel for what the reception of a letter meant then. You don't kiss emails or digital photos. We may try to read the books and poems Lilo and Ernst read, to sing or listen to the songs that formed their cultural world, and to look at their films, but our *blik* (perspective) is so very different. We are a flighty, twittering generation. We have little in our experience comparable to the rich seams of this protracted and intimate correspondence. We have also learned to live with pluralism and relativism. It is hard to enter this "intact" world, with its full-blooded convictions.

What we can recognize, however, is that it was their photos, their letters and postcards, and their parcels (big ones at times, enclosing apples, or clothes, or cakes) which kept both of them going, which held the bond of love firm. We have 1,026 of these letters and cards, from 1935 to Ernst's death on the Russian Front near Staraja Russa in 1942. Many of the photos from the photo albums are also extant. Ernst mailed more than twice as many letters and postcards to Lilo as she did to him, which is surprising. However, many of his are postcards, virtually none of hers. She also dispatched many more parcels.

"Post, post that is everything." When the postman came, Lilo's two-year-old daughter would shout, "Pappi!"[9] The mailman delivered what for Lilo was her "daily bread." The mail from the Front was her *Heiligtum* (shrine or sanctuary).[10] These love letters gave her new impetus and fresh courage. Ernst's letters, parcels, and picture cards to the children were rapturously received. When he was in training in Lübeck, they were able to reach one

---

9. *Post, Post, das ist alles*. Lilo to Ernst, January 28, 1941: parcels went both ways; Ernst often sent clothes, presents, and food to Lilo and the children.

10. Lilo to Ernst, August 12, 1941.

another several times on the phone as well, but letters were the real lifeline. Unfortunately we have to imagine the parcels, wrapped up and packed with such love, and received by both partners with such appreciation: the chocolates, the cigarettes, the candles, and the pipe; countless cakes, the apples from the garden; and the smoked sausage; from France; the shoes, dates, figs, oranges, lemons, nuts, and toys for the children![11] Not to forget, either, the packages of washed and lovingly ironed clothes sent back by Lilo. Hard, incidentally, not to be impressed by the efficiency of the German postal service, civil and military!

Undoubtedly Lilo hero-worshiped Ernst. It was music to her ears to hear from his comrades that he looked *blühend* (radiant). He had, she felt, such a "wonderful temperament and a magnificent, healthy, fit body. You are a wonderful human being. Ernst, I am so proud of you. . . ." Yet this did not inhibit her criticisms. Having seen the notes in his diary, for example, she knew that he headed off on his own through the Russian woods on his motorbike, used attics and towers for observation purposes, and often only managed to evade danger at the last moment. "*Schwein gehabt* (Gosh, I was lucky!)," he would say.[12] Her repeatedly voiced worries about his rash disregard of snipers are a good example of her doubts about his judgement, his set of priorities. She let him know precisely what she thought. She was her own person.

While Ernst fell head over heels for Lilo, he did not reciprocate that hero-worship. She was his dear, *little* wife, while for Lilo he was her *big* boy.[13] Ernst operated within traditional gender parameters. Their relationship was a complex one. She was his refuge when he was troubled and a source of strength, but she was also, almost in the pedagogical sense of that word, his *Aufgabe* (task).[14] There was a pedantic streak to him. Lilo, too, took that for granted. He was the teacher, with an *Abitur* (university entrance) and a tertiary education behind him. She was fortunate enough to be his pupil.

They sent off letters to pass on the latest news about the children or money problems, about the daily round, and about visits from other family

11. Lilo to Ernst, January 11, 1941; for a while a weight limit was imposed on parcels, so clothes or fruit could not be sent; but Lilo was able in October to send parcels of two pounds; Lilo to Ernst, October 24, 1941; a parcel of crisp apples was a particular hit; Ernst to Lilo, November 11, 1941.

12. Lilo to Ernst, September 20, 1941.

13. *Du liebe, gute, süße, kleine Soldatenfrau*; Ernst to Lilo, November 24, 1939.

14. Ernst to Lilo, May 21, 1940.

The Special Significance of the Letters

members. More significantly the aim was to offer reassurance, to share happiness, or at the other end of the spectrum, to let off steam. Letters certainly brought a surge of joy, were a "ray of sunshine." Each newly arrived letter, addressed with the familiar hand, was a cause for *Feier* (celebration) and was hailed with *Rausch* (ecstasy). For Ernst Lilo's handwriting was like a kiss.[15] ("No typing please," he pled with her!)

On New Year's Eve 1939 Lilo wrote:

Dear, good Ernst, I know that there are so few like you. I am so proud of you and so infinitely grateful for the wealth and the love which have come into my life through you. . . . Thank you for your loving words [she wrote in early 1940], I need your letters as much as I need air to breathe. They are all I have of you. Your words touch my heart, they mean everything to me. I'm like a young girl in love, full of the joy of life. When you write lovingly to me I have to shut my eyes, it just burns me up.[16]

Letters could also cause alarm, though. Once Lilo got a frightful shock when a letter arrived with the address on the back bearing the name of Lt. Magerhans, one of his fellow officers. Stricken, and convinced it was a report on Ernst's death, she resolutely refused to open it. It turned out, when she eventually relented, that Magerhans had just been acting as courier.[17] When there was no letter for a week or more, Lilo always feared the worst.[18]

The letters and photos from home, the accounts of the children's first words,[19] their learning to crawl and walk, their illnesses—whooping cough, worms, colds, measles—and the accounts of their exploits and adventures in house and garden, allowed Ernst to forget for a while the life at the Front. They gave him a vision of another world, of home and its wonderful peace, of "Paradise." There is a sinister dimension to this. For they also played a

---

15. Ernst to Lilo, June 12, 1940; cf. also July 28, 1940.
16. Lilo to Ernst, January 6, 1940.
17. Lilo to Ernst, December 10, 1941.
18. "How can one be brave when one fears for the person dearest to one?" Lilo to Ernst, April 7, 1941.
19. Lilo told Ernst that Heinke's first words were: *Papa, Herta, Hartmut*; a cow was *muhmuh*; a horse *huhu*; oranges *balla balla*; looking at a photo, she said to Ella Butenschön: "There's Mama, Heinke, Hartmut; Pappi, too? No! What a pity! Ach, doesn't matter, he'll be back soon." Heinke would also try to coach her little brother, Hartmut: " Say, 'Mama'; say 'Papa.'" Lilo to Ernst, June 30, 1940; January 23, 1941; October 17, 1941; November 4, 1941.

part in permitting him to continue to idealize the invasion of Russia, as allegedly its aim was to safeguard and extend that "paradise."

Lilo sometimes wrote late into the night, and Ernst continued to write even in the midst of the fiercest fighting, at least a postcard; occasionally he scribbled a note while riding his horse or lying on his stomach on the front line. Sometimes in now very illegible pencil. Lilo knew how fortunate she was to be the recipient of such frequent and loving letters; it was as if they were still young lovers, not a sedately married couple.[20]

They never forgot the special days, anniversaries, birthdays, Whitsun, or Easter; before Christmas veritable avalanches of letters and parcels were sent off. Ernst's brother; his brother-in-law, Dieter; his sisters; his mother; and other friends and family wrote him as well as Lilo. The fourth of August was Lilo's birthday. She reflected that she was now twenty-eight, and had got to know Ernst when she was twenty-two. Six wonderful years![21] The volume of letters witnesses to the intensity of that wonder and love. Where possible Lilo should use the ordinary mail service, Ernst urged, for it was quicker than the military post. "I desperately need your long letters." He urged her never to write less than two pages. They swept him into the world of his *holde* (noble) wife and lovely children, and of his village home.[22]

They both became furious and even desperate when delays in the post occurred; Ernst would express his joy and relief when several letters arrived at once. He could also be quite upset if he didn't hear at once, say, about the illness of one of the children.[23] They talked of *verschlingen* (devouring) the letters when they eventually arrived. The letters were eaten, so to speak, were their nourishment, their food.

Ernst's solicitude for wife and children was thoughtful, and very touching. He always wanted to know straightaway, after she visited him, that she had got home safely, that changing trains had not been too difficult; every detail was important to him.[24] We profit today from his pedantry. Ernst also on occasion showed off his considerable understanding of child psychology.[25]

20. Lilo to Ernst, November 20, 1941.
21. Lilo to Ernst, August 3, 1941.
22. Ernst to Lilo, May 16, 1941.
23. Ernst to Lilo, September 23, 1939; October 7, 1939.
24. Ernst to Lilo, November 14, 1939.
25. Ernst to Lilo, November 14, 1939.

The Special Significance of the Letters

They could be very direct with one another. If Ernst did not respond to a specific question, or if she thought the letter a bit skimpy Lilo would complain forcibly;[26] if clothes sent on by him for her or the children were too big or too small, he got that message, too. On an altogether more serious level she warned him not to go chasing the Iron Cross like Hans. She had just heard of Hans's injury.[27]

Ernst noted that although he sometimes felt "caressed" by her words, that was by no means always the case. "Your letters are certainly always loving and kind, but sometimes quite impossible. Only lovers can write like that, you sweet thing, you."[28] He wearied at times of her conflicts with other members of his family. "If only you could put away all pettiness and live only for and out of our love I would be so happy."[29] He urged her, for his sake, caught as he was between the two women, to make her peace with his mother.[30] He also found it painfully difficult that Lilo was so jealous of Gerda, Hans's wife, and that she imagined that Ernst was smitten by her as well.[31]

Lilo was aware that she caused him trouble:

> Are you less than happy with my letters, and do they make it harder for you to keep going? Is it that I let myself go, and moan and groan too much? I'm sorry, Ernst, it's probably because I am used to letting you in on all my most intimate reactions and feelings. In my letters I shake out my whole heart to you always and shun any kind of mask.[32]

She certainly did.

The letters were read and reread as they lay down in their separate beds at night. Both set apart time, especially in the evening, to imagine what it would be like if the other were present. The detailed descriptions of every moment of daily life, whether at home or on the Front, facilitated this. They "held colloquy" with the framed photographs of their partner. Both had the ability to write from the heart, moving the other to tears or to joy, confident

26. Lilo to Ernst, February 9, 1941.
27. Lilo to Ernst, August 3, 1941.
28. Ernst to Lilo, November 20, 1939.
29. Ernst to Lilo, October 22, 1940; *Daß auch Du alles Kleine abtun könntest und nur unserer Liebe und aus ihr leben würdest, ist mein Wunsch.*
30. Ernst to Lilo, January 20, 1940.
31. Ernst to Lilo, June 9, 1941.
32. Lilo to Ernst, September 20, 1941.

of their mutual love and passion.[33] The photos that the lieutenant proudly displayed in hut or dugout of his wife and children were a piece of home, admired by visitors and by his men. At the same time, they both knew that letters could never make up for the real thing, being together.[34]

They deployed a great variety of names when addressing one another. In his letters Ernst called Lilo "my golden lass"; "Schnucki, Schnukilein" ("cutie, little cutie"); "little one"; "my happiness on earth, the pivot of my being"; and "my support, the driving force of my life." Lilo in turn called Ernst "Butzi" ("my dear big boy"), "my dearest," "my beloved," and "my most beloved Ernst." The emotional drive of their language was more significant than its originality. They described their love as deep, unique, irreplaceable, unconditional, a profound community of spirit, and at times didn't hesitate to write in fiery, erotic terms. They were homesick for one another and longed for their joy in life, their *Lebenslust* (their delight in one another), to blossom freely once again.

Lilo, however, could also talk quite freely of *angst*, of this ghastly, mad, and accursed war, and both of them could speak of exhaustion, of spiritual distress, of depression, and of yearning. Their language can be rather fruity and at times borders on the sentimental. Ernst's talk of *heißem Erschauern und stiller Andacht,* for example, is hard to render into English, something like "shuddering awe and profound reverence."

In autumn 1941 as the Russian campaign ground on, Ernst's loving letters lifted her spirits, and kindled memories of the time when they first met and became engaged. "That wonderful time when we got close to one another, so uniquely and so profoundly."[35] They relived their past, and looked forward to their future as they swapped letters about the present.

The war had torn them apart, and the primary function of their letters, postcards, and parcels was to challenge this tyranny of distance. This was true, of course, for innumerable other couples on both sides of the war. Countless wives and mothers received the dreaded message about their partner "missing in action" and had to wait for an eternity to hear

---

33. Cf. Lilo's letter of December 25, 1940: *Die Sehnsucht ist so groß und das Blut singt und strömt und ein übervolles Herz muß sich Luft machen.* (My yearning is so strong, my blood sings and floods my body, and my thumping heart has to find a way to express all this.) She weeps into her cushion, and longs to lose herself totally in his kisses and his embrace.

34. Ernst to Lilo, February 3, 1940: *Man kann nie die Wirklichkeit durch Briefe ersetzen.*

35. Lilo to Ernst, September 18, 1941.

the worst, or to be somewhat relieved by the news that their partner was in the hospital or in a prisoner-of-war camp. Down the ages ballads and folk songs remind us that war and the heartbreak of separation always go hand in hand.

The priorities of war had made nonsense of Ernst and Lilo's personal and also professional agendas. Moreover, for all their unmistakable affection for one another, differences in temperament made it difficult for them from the very beginning. In September 1939 Ernst wrote to his "dear, good Lilo," full of sympathy for her lonely days and nights. Yet he found consolation in reflecting that countless other comrades shared the same fate of separation from wife and child. Some, admittedly, used connections and corruption to avoid being conscripted:

> Darling, forget these people. For my part, I would not care to sleep on comfortable beds while my comrades prove their manly courage at the Front. I know that women have the worst of it, but we don't go into battle irresponsibly, either. I am aware of my duties, so that my conscience can be at ease. I carry [my duties] out joyfully and I know that in your heart you agree with me. Better to have a dead husband than a coward.[36]

Lilo would have found scant consolation in that thought.

The tyranny of distance between them was in part, of course, geographical. After they had fallen in love, they had been forced into a two-year-long engagement and their respective homes in Schleswig-Holstein and Pomerania lay at opposite ends of the country. They shared married life together in Wrohm only for one short year. Then as month succeeded month they had to sustain a relationship in which they almost never saw each other. This distance was a continuing torture. They used imaginative metaphors to try to overcome it. When he left her, Ernst said, he took her heart with him in the car, in the train; in camp he could still hear it beating for him, the most devoted heart in the world.

Yet together with the geographical distance there developed a growing cultural estrangement, too. Lilo was aware that her man lived in a quite different world from hers. The uniformed world clashed with the civilian world, the military with the domestic, and the comradeship of the men with the lonely life at home. It was painful for Lilo to realize that she knew virtually nothing of this other world, that his preoccupations were quite alien to her. Ernst and his comrades traveled in cars, still a rare commodity;

---

36. Ernst to Lilo, September 3, 1939.

in France they rode horses through distant landscapes. Their world was extensive; her women's world was bounded by house and garden. Her own longings to see a wider world remained thwarted.[37] Ernst, too, was aware of this growing chasm between their lives, but he could affirm his military training and engagement in a wholehearted way. That became less and less possible for Lilo. He had agency, was often quite literally on the move; she felt deserted and stranded.

For both of them, the separation was worst during the pregnancy and birth of their second child, though Ernst's mother was there, and despite previous tensions between wife and mother-in-law proved a "fabulous" help.[38] Always particularly painful was the separation at Christmastime, such a tradition- and emotion-laden feast in Germany. In 1940 Lilo set apart the whole of Christmas Eve to focus on Ernst. She described the scene to him in glowing detail, the tree with its sparkling lametta, and the toys for the children, including building blocks, toy carts, a doll, and mountains of sweets and clothes.[39] When his Christmas letter arrived, though, "all my bravery collapsed. I just want to hold on to our happiness, not to make sacrifices; my blood sings and my heart spills over; how I'd love to be kissed and to sink into you. I know you feel the same." She held his photo in her hand and talked to it, as if it were her personal icon, and thought of the dear, sweet children, the fruit of their marriage. She had to cry as she sang the Christmas carol: "O du fröhliche"("O How Joyful"), for she had hoped against hope that he might get leave to join them.[40]

This protracted waiting and *Ungewissheit* (uncertainty) was the worst aspect of the separation. Hoping, praying, and waiting, as she put it. Waiting for him to get leave. Again and again leave was promised, but seldom eventuated. In 1941 she had been hugely looking forward to him coming at Whitsun, and it was all planned. By a miracle it did work out at the last moment. Unknown to her, however, the preparations for the Russian offensive were already underway. Leave would then become a thing of the past.[41]

Letter after letter testifies to her sense of vertiginous helplessness, of having fallen into an abyss of depression or angry resignation. Waiting for a letter to prove he was still well, or at least alive, proved a constant strain

37. Lilo to Ernst, January 11, 1941.
38. Lilo to Ernst, March 29, 1940.
39. Lilo to Ernst, December 25, 1940.
40. Lilo to Ernst, December 25, 1940.
41. Lilo to Ernst, April 30, 1941.

on her all-too-vivid imagination. With each day's delay in the arrival of the post her anxiety grew. Whenever a few days went by without a letter, her instinct told her that it was all over with Ernst. She waited in mounting desperation for every postal delivery. But nothing came! She needed constant reassurance, and rode a rollercoaster of emotions.

She did not hesitate to pass these on to Ernst. Wearing her heart on her sleeve in their relations to one another had become second nature to her. Her fervently expressed love for Ernst morphed into terror for him, for his children, and for all their dreams of a life together. She unloaded all this onto him.

As Lilo saw it the individual person, Ernst, was being sacrificed to the *Volk*, although she never articulated this perception in so many words. She did recognize that her *angst* was hard on him, yet the thought that he might be utterly thrown, taken aback, and dismayed by her depression and alarm came as a rude shock. She does not seem to have realized that her outbursts shell-shocked Ernst, that they had a traumatic effect on their recipient.[42] Perhaps she overestimated his capacity to cope, forgetting that empathy flowed in both directions. Of course, behind these personal tensions lay the collision of two different worlds, that of family and that of the war machine. That is the significance of these letters. They testify to the frank, determined, distressed, and distressing attempt of two passionate lovers to maintain communication across impossible frontiers.

Towards the end of Ernst's life the *Postsperre* (ban on letters), due to the need to get ammunition and other supplies up to meet the Russian counteroffensive, accentuated Lilo's agony. Her heart bled, as she put it. She indulged in quite unrealistic hopes. Against her better knowledge that those on the Russian Front were not to be relieved, she would check each bus as it arrived in Spantekow in case after all Ernst had got leave for Christmas in 1941.[43]

She quite definitely gave a heartfelt and genuine welcome to news of the army's victories. When the *Sondermeldungen* boomed out (the pompous radio announcements preceded by the Prinz Eugen fanfare or the *Deutschlandlied*), she had tears in her eyes. The fall of Belgrade, for example, filled her with pride and elation. Yet a disconnect emerged between her affirmation of the Reich's military campaigns and her attitude to those battles in which Ernst was personally involved, and in which he

---

42. Lilo to Ernst, September 17, 1941.
43. . . . *mir blutet das Herz*; Lilo to Ernst, December 17, 1941.

faced danger. Moreover, "as a woman I am ... always aware of the sacrifices, privations, the *Entbehrungen* (hard yards), needed to get there."[44] She was a realist, and was not taken in by the drumbeat of the propaganda.

The worst aspect for her about being on the so-called Home Front was the waiting for an end to an apparently endless war, a war that kept escalating and expanding into the furthest reaches of Europe and beyond. Waiting, too, for an end to the bombing raids by the "Tommies," as she crouched with the kids in the dark cellar, listening to the howl of the bombs, the din made by the air defenses. She felt betrayed by the bombing of Kiel. It was just not acceptable. How could the "Tommies" go on destroying German cities? "I think we have to get over to England and shut their mouths." The delay in the invasion of England, the "head of the snake," made no sense to her.[45] There is an unacknowledged criticism here of the empty boasts of a Göring and his buddies.

"I hang between the tree and the bark," as she put it in a haunting metaphor. She was as anxious as Ernst was confident, or appeared to be. He had always had the gift, she felt, of adapting himself to whatever fate threw his way.[46] The future was full of unknowns and alarms for her. Ernst had his comrades around him. In Wrohm Lilo was very much alone, and the long winter evenings dragged. One moment she was up, happy and fulfilled; the next she was down, and haunted by fears, real and unreal. As early as the beginning of 1940 she was voicing her sense of depression: "Without you everything is empty, one day is like the next, I live without any sense of time or goal." She was to continue to struggle against depression.[47] As the war stretched on, she felt increasingly disempowered, unsatisfied, and redundant, like a field that is *brach* (fallow).[48]

After three years of war and separation from Ernst, she felt by spring 1941 that she had "had it." She was absolutely sick of being alone, of a life with nothing to it but work and children. She was hungry for life, for company, for joie de vivre. It was at day's ending that she missed him most: "There's no joy to life anymore."[49]

44. Lilo to Ernst, April 13, 1941; April 11, 1941.
45. Lilo to Ernst, April 15, 1941; April 17, 1941.
46. Lilo to Ernst, January 14, 1940.
47. Lilo to Ernst, January 6, 1940; January 26, 1941.
48. Lilo to Ernst, June 1, 1940; October 27, 1941.
49. Lilo to Ernst, October 24, 1941.

The Special Significance of the Letters

Ernst's veil of silence about future military actions disquieted her. What did it mean that his unit was moving stealthily eastwards, she asked in the spring of 1941? Was the nonaggression pact with Russia not *sicher* (reliable), she wondered? Everyone was aware of the huge massing of troops in East Prussia.[50] By 1941 she was sure that it would not be a quick war. America would soon be involved. "The whole world is in flames."[51] Her questions were good, her apprehensions valid enough.

The long separation heightened their longing to "fly to the other's breast." Lilo became dizzy, just thinking about it. She could acknowledge at times that in some ways it was much harder for him. She at least had the children. Both talk again and again of their longing to be together again, to kiss, stroke one another's hair, and be there for each other in body and mind and soul.[52] To be close, to be one flesh.

Writing from Staraja Russa on December 6, 1941, Ernst faced the fact that for the third time they would be celebrating Christmas apart:

> *But there's nothing for it. [Bringing up supplies and ammunition for the winter months had the priority over provision for leave.] I am far, far from you in the endless reaches of Russia, yet am so close to you. [He pictured the candlelit Christmas tree in all its glory, the eyes of the children, wide open in wonder. He imagined the overflowing heart of his big girl (she is not yet three!) breaking out in joy and singing. The teacher in him was aware that Heinke would already be taking in the magic of it all. He has just been involved in fierce battle, but] . . . My heart is so marvelously at peace when I think of you. The good Lord has preserved me thus far for my dear ones. We both want to come together in thankfulness and prayer.*

What separated them were not just the hundreds and hundreds of kilometers but the desolation of his environment, the qualitative difference: "here everything is cold and white, vast and empty, poor and sad, burnt out, shot to pieces"; compared with this they lived in a quite different world, dreamlike in its beauty, a fairy-tale beauty, almost a paradise.[53]

His very last letter, only two days before he was shot in the stomach and killed, thanked her for the first letters of 1942 and for the photos:

50. Lilo to Ernst, April 17, 1941; April 21, 1941.
51. Lilo to Ernst, January 11, 1941.
52. Lilo to Ernst, June 4, 1941.
53. Ernst to Lilo, December 16, 1941.

> *My darling, Hurrah! The first letters from you in the New Year. I am assured of your love and your yearning. I am so happy about that. How lovingly you wrote. Dearest, please write by hand. I don't like typewritten letters. Will you be so kind? It seems the post is on stream again. That is wonderful. I'll write a proper letter soon. There is time enough for it. I am well. The sweet pictures delighted me, but I miss you so. You are the pivot of all my longings.*
> *In deepest love, I am*
> *Your Ernst.*[54]

In many ways, not least because of their density of detail, their frankness and their skill with language, and their two-way traffic, these letters open a poignant window into the lives and perspectives of the "little people" in Nazi Germany, the personal tragedy that was unfolding behind the drama of world-shaking events. Passionate about each other, they were also passionate about Hitler's coming Reich. They were both idealists. Inch by inch, however, letter by letter, we see their idealism being unraveled. Inch by inch we see them facing up to this.

Such letters have the vividness but also the limitations of all *Egodokumente* (personal papers), and have to be put into context. The correspondence of Ernst and Lilo has to be seen side by side, with that, say, of Bonhoeffer, and of all those who took the lonely alternative of resisting the regime. It has to be seen in the context of books such as Saul Friedländer's *Nazi Germany and the Jews*, of Walter Kempowski's collective diary, *Das Echolot* (*The Sounding Line*), and of the devastating realism of Nicholas Stargardt's *The German War*.[55] The German poet Hölderlin described human life not just as being in *Gespräch* (conversation) but *as* conversation.[56] The question, in regard to Ernst and Lilo, might run, conversation with whom? Who was excluded from their conversation? How narrow was their world? Not least because these young parents appear as caring, well-meaning people, this correspondence raises endless and inescapable questions about the relationship between the personal and the political, about the costs of youthful idealism and its cynical exploitation by those in power, and about the limitations of insight and of human agency.

54. Ernst to Lilo, February 10, 1942.

55. Friedländer, *Nazi Germany and the Jews*; Kempowski, *Das Echolot*; Stargardt, *The German War*; Littell, *The Kindly Ones* is a brilliant, unremitting novel about the brutalities and horror of the Russian campaign.

56. "Seit ein Gespräch wir sind und hören voneinander"; from Hölderlin's poem "Celebration of Peace" (*Friedensfeier*).

Conclusion

It is difficult at times to repress the thought that history is about as instructive as an abattoir.
—SEAMUS HEANEY, 1995

THE ISSUES THROWN OPEN by this correspondence are complex, in the end of the day intractable. How can one do justice to the humanity of these young lovers and parents, still in their twenties, while keeping firmly in mind the landscape of brutality and horror that was unravelling, and of which they were a part? How are we to make sense of any of it? Or, as Seamus Heaney wonders, is that the wrong question?

Seventy to eighty years later it is difficult for us to imagine how reality was filtered to those living in the Third Reich, not only through overt propaganda and censorship, but through family traditions and prejudices, and real and imagined hurts from the past, by children's books, by the maps on the school wall, by folk songs and catchy music on the radio, and by romantic novels and nationalistic histories. Increasingly much of the educational literature for schools was full of racist undertones and overtones. Even notepaper and envelopes could have slogans such as: "You, woman of Germany, are the support of the fighter on the front line."[1]

It is true that popular songs, which Lilo loved, such as "Hörst Du mein heimliches Rufen?" ("Can You Hear My Hidden Cry?") or indeed the music of Lili Marlene, had a melancholy quality that could subvert its propagandistic use. On the whole, however, Goebbels's propaganda onslaught had formidable success. The upmarket periodical *Das Reich* was on Ernst's

---

1. *Den Kämpfer der Front stützt Du, deutsche Frau, daheim.* Paul Struck to Lilo, November 8, 1939.

wish list. Press and radio were firmly controlled. The Party newspaper, the *Völkischer Beobachter*, was widely read. Millions of posters were circulated. Theaters, slideshows, and films played a key part.[2] Not all was ideological, of course; like everyone else Lilo and Ernst enjoyed the occasional escapist film.

But the *Wochenschau* (newsreel), often a triumphalist documentary on the progress of the war, which was shown before feature films, was hugely popular. Both Ernst and Lilo saw the highly successful film *Jud Süss*, the depiction of an eighteenth-century Jewish moneylender who was hanged for crimes including the seduction of a German woman. Ernst commented that he found it *in Ordnung* (okay). Even in little Wrohm a cinema showed propaganda films. Snatches of church piety remained, especially around Easter, Whitsun, and Christmas, and some young people still attended confirmation classes, but for most people Christianity had been excluded from the public realm.

Books and films and radio were one thing. Still more influential, perhaps, were the rituals of daily life, the *Heil Hitler* that began the school day, the collecting for innumerable National Socialist causes, attendance at Hitler Youth or Young Women's meetings, women's sewing groups, SA marches and torchlight processions, and celebrations such as the *Heldengedenktag* (the cult of the heroic dead in past wars). The swastika and portraits of the Führer were omnipresent.

Unlike those higher up in society, travel or contacts overseas were unthinkable for Ernst and Lilo, although Ernst did get away briefly to Belgium and Denmark with his Hitler Youth boys. Access to accurate, independent information about the political and military situation was out of the question for them. Lacking a trade union or social democratic or communist affiliation, they had virtually no alternative perspectives to draw upon.[3] Many of the questions we would want to ask did not even surface for them. The secondary virtues of duty, orderliness, and discipline exerted a power unthinkable today.

---

2. In some films, such as *Der ewige Jud (The Eternal Jew)*, the propaganda was too blatant to be successful; Ernst saw several films during his time in Potsdam, including *Der Postmeister (The Postmaster)*, apparently revealing the brutality of the Russian soul; the stars, Heinrich George and Hilde Krahl were famous; Ernst to Lilo, June 18, 1940. Films were shown as part of the program of the War Academy in Potsdam.

3. The comparison with Anna Haag's extensive feminist, socialist, and pacifist networks is illuminating; Timms, *Anna Haag and Her Secret Diary*, esp. 49–54.

Conclusion

Ernst and Lilo Sommer were followers, not leaders. In many ways they were typical of many ordinary people who were swept along by the tides of their time. The cultural consensus among their family members and colleagues, long before the blitzkrieg campaigns in Poland and France, was that an exciting, heroic new future lay ahead for Germany. One has to remember that every major pillar of German society had capitulated to National Socialist power and ideology: the judiciary, the universities, the schools, the civil service, the military, the media, and to a large extent the churches. The papacy had signed a concordat with the Reich in 1933, one-third of Protestant clergy and laity had thrown in their lot with National Socialist racism, and the limited resistance of the Confessing Church on issues of theology and church independence did not impinge on the Sommer family. If they knew of the harassment and imprisonment of priests and ministers, there is no hint of it in their letters.

Germany's honor and freedom were the causes that caught them by the throat, and were symbolized by the swastika flags, and choreographed in the great Nuremberg Rallies. They believed in the genius of the Führer, and his rhetoric swept them off their feet. Ernst's mother wrote in February 1938 that she had been so held *ganz im Bann* (captivated) by a three-hour speech by the Führer, transmitted by radio, that she had to go for a long walk in the sunshine to calm herself after listening to it.[4] Hitler spoke to their hearts.

All this happened some seventy years ago, yet the words leap from the pages of these letters as if they were written yesterday. This is partly because of their intimacy; the letters were meant for no other eyes than theirs. There are, as mentioned at the outset, ethical issues here. Have we any right to read them? Is such a violation of their privacy, their pain and distress justified?

One attempts to read them without either censoriousness or the will to exculpate. These letters illumine vividly the tragedy of war, the depth and wonder of human love, and the helplessness and limited awareness of ordinary people when swept into such conflagrations. Both sword and fiddle feature here, the resort to brutal violence and the dream of a cultured and loving home. Over the centuries Germany had developed an incomparable heritage of music, poetry, art, and literature;, and Ernst and Lilo were anything but unaware of that. But home is such an ambivalent concept. Was it Ernst's and Lilo's very love of *Heimat* (home), one wonders,

---

4. Ernst to Leni, February 20, 1938.

that drove them into the arms of Hitler? It is a theme constantly evoked in their songbooks. It was the conviction that he was defending this precious, sacred home against the ravages of Bolshevism that sustained Ernst on the Russian Front.

The closer one moves into the day-to-day life in the Third Reich, the harder it is to form sweeping judgements, whether intellectual, political, moral, or theological. One has to be cautious of course about generalizing too much from the actions and attitudes of Ernst and Lilo, about setting them up as average, representative exemplars of the "little people." For they were also, in various ways, extraordinary, or at least unusual. The exceptionally rich vein of their correspondence is one clear indicator of that.[5] Ernst was an unusually talented teacher, and a fine officer. He talks on several occasions of his sense of alienation from other officers. Lilo, too, was "different." For all her *angst*, she had rare strength of character, called a spade a spade, was an exemplary mother, was her own person, and asked herself many of the right questions about the war, about the nature of faith.

We have also to remember that the evidence provided by this correspondence is partial. Much remains unknown to us, and is not revealed by the letters. What did Ernst see of the violation of human rights in the French campaign? What do we make, for example, of the presents he sent back from there, in common with all his comrades, which emptied the shelves and drove up prices for ordinary French people? There is a significant silence about the *Einsatzgruppen* (special detachments) in his letters from the Russian campaign, about those death squads that herded up Jews, political opponents, and intellectuals in the wake of the army's advances. There is no mention of the concentration camp in Graudenz. The German army as a whole was involved in Poland and Russia in unspeakable atrocities against women and children, and innocent civilians.[6] It is clear that the *Wehrmacht* (army) was involved in the collective punishment of innocent villagers, pursued "partisans" indiscriminately, and cooperated with the SS. It has therefore been described by distinguished historians as an instrument of genocide. Our sources are silent about the extent of Ernst Sommer's involvement in such atrocities, apart from references to fighting the

---

5. Talking of the difficulty of evaluating memoirs and diaries for social history Vinen comments: "Autobiographies by 'ordinary' people can of course be deceptive. A peasant who keeps a diary or writes a memoir is less typical of his milieu than a lycée *professeur*." Vinen, *The Unfree French*, 8. (For Ernst, as we have seen, the letters had become his diary.)

6. Evans, *The Third Reich at War*, 3–108; Stargardt, *The German War*, esp. 165–98.

Conclusion

partisans.[7] Was Ernst's reticence typical of the subtle silence so pervasive in the Third Reich? He did talk occasionally of becoming "hard," which can be a code term for complicity in inhumane conduct. Even the official division history, after all, speaks of the "unavoidably rigorous treatment of the local inhabitants and prisoners of war."[8] On the other hand, Lilo did say in reference to one of the French prisoners in her village. "It is hard to see the prisoners as enemies. We women see the human being there."[9] One should be cautious about assuming that Ernst had no similar feelings about Russian civilians.

Hannah Arendt regards a homelessness of spirit as one of the grounds for the success of totalitarianism in capturing the minds and hearts of ordinary people.[10] Yet is this evident in this instance? Both Ernst and Lilo, on the face of it, seem deeply rooted in their time and place, if anything far too deeply rooted. Those of us who have benefited from a long democratic tradition tend to forget that in the German churches, as much as in civil culture, authoritarian models of governance were regarded as the healthy ones.

What, then, explains the susceptibility of Ernst and Lilo and of their families to National Socialism? These letters raise the question rather than answer it. There is no evidence that they ever considered any alternatives to it. What are we to make of the role of religion or of the high sense of duty in their lives? What sort of Christianity was theirs, what aspects of National Socialism did they warm to? Again, we have to be cautious about assuming that they did not criticize aspects of it. Ernst continued to advocate for the confirmation of his young pupils in church. Lilo excoriated excessive sentimentality about land and soil. On the margins, at least, they had their criticisms, though nothing was said against its violence and racism and ethnocentrism. Personally, there is much to admire in them, yet paradoxically it was the tender and ardent love of his wife that enabled Ernst to endure, and thus participate in, the inhumanity of Operation Barbarossa.

---

7. Occasionally Ernst's letters talk about him riding on his horse, Titus, through the woods, Ernst to Lilo 12 September 1941; but specific information about possible clashes with partisans is missing, probably because Lilo worried about snipers in the woods and urged him not to go on these expeditions; his letters only offer any detail about the direct confrontations with the Russian army.

8. . . . *unumgängliche Härte gegen Landeinwohner und Gefangene*; Bauer, 290. *Infanterie Division. Weg und Schicksal*, 124.

9. Lilo to Ernst, February 2, 1941.

10. Arendt, *The Origins of Totalitarianism*, xxix.

These letters encourage us to juxtapose the human reality of their love with the brutality of the war. Lilo and Ernst were clear that they belonged together, for better or for worse, till death did them part. Although they were in no way exceptionally gifted, culturally or intellectually, pen and ink enabled them to transcend the barriers that separated and threatened to alienate them. The continual pain and frustration, so evident in these letters, is the flip side to the intensity of their love. The Russian campaign had hardened Ernst, as he recognized, yet the flow of letters enabled him to preserve something of his gentleness, warmth, and empathy at least as far as wife and family were concerned. Likewise the war wrecked Lilo's composure, but the vividness, concreteness, and emotional wealth of the letters kept her on her feet as mother and carer, and enabled her, ultimately, to rebuild her life after the war. Virtually everything else in her life may have fallen victim to Nazism. The reality of their love for one another survived.

Afterword: A Personal Pilgrimage

BY PURE ACCIDENT *I heard in May 2001 that my brother, Hartmut, intended to join an army veterans' group traveling to Russia, to Saint Petersburg and Novgorod, to attend the dedication of a new war cemetery in Korpowo, to visit other cemeteries, and to honor the fallen of both nations. He mentioned the proposed trip in a phone call. This came as a bolt from the blue. In far-off New Zealand I had limited access to Hartmut's thinking and plans; I knew him as a keen traveler who had often set off for Italy, Greece, and North Africa, but I had no idea at all that he was in touch with the veterans' association, and was keen to trace his father's footsteps in Russia. As it happened, he had come across in his housing block in Neu-Ulm an ex-army officer, and then talked with him about the Russian campaign, though it was an emotional business for the latter to revisit the memories from the war. This officer had connections with Herr von Mackensen, who was organizing what would be the last chance for these now elderly veterans to journey to the war graves. I knew instantaneously that I had to be part of this expedition, and to Hartmut's utter surprise insisted on it. So within a couple of months, I arranged a flight to Germany, Hartmut generously financing it all.*

Initially I saw it as eine Entdeckungsreise *(a voyage of discovery), following the trail of the father I had never known. Ever since I learned that he had been killed in Russia I had been puzzled, and wanted to know more. I needed to dispel my ignorance about that land, and about the Russians, and above all about my father's last days there. Being there, perhaps finding his grave, would help to remove the mystique that had surrounded him since my childhood. He would become a real person for me. Later I was to understand what this whole journey actually meant to me; it was to be a pilgrimage, a journey in space and time, and a sacred duty.*

I also needed to do justice to my mother. All the support she had found in Ernst had disappeared when he died; she only gradually became her own person again. I wondered who my mother confided in, then, and after the war. What a struggle for naked survival she had! Lilo had been close to Ernst's loyal associate teacher, Elsa Butenschön, but she was now far away in Pinneberg. Maybe her relatives, Inge and Hans-Joachim Friedrich, were closest to being her confidants? Without a man at her side she felt inadequate, and kept her distance from friends like the Corsepius family. My cousin, Hannelore, daughter of Ernst's sister, Tudi, may well have summed up her feelings: "I think there's a curse on our family; all its men have died in the war."

Lilo had become so full of inhibitions. She felt she was not good enough or bright enough. No one advised her to complete her education, train as a pharmacist, for example. It became clear to me that for none of us, Mutti, myself, or Hartmut, did the war end in 1945. It had marked us for life.

The Lilo I encountered in the letters was also, though, a very determined, capable woman, quite unlike the vulnerable war widow I knew in my student days in Bonner Talweg, where she was intimidated and terrorized by her landlord, an ex-SA man.

It was difficult to prepare myself. On a previous visit to my mother's flat in the Londonerstraße in Bonn I had once found Hartmut and Lilo mulling over the history of my father's regiment; and my mother had taken some of her letters to my father out of a brown box, and seeing my interest had sent me one of his letters to her on my birthday; but I had not the least awareness of the extent of the correspondence.

My reading about the invasion of Russia, and about the experiences of the bewildered generation who had lost their fathers as I had, about the political and racialist policies of Hitler, all was to follow this expedition. They flowed from it. I had no time or opportunity to do this before setting out.

Emotionally, though, I knew the journey would be harrowing. I would be trying to locate a father who had been absent from my life since I was three years old, and simultaneously I would have to find a way to say goodbye to him. I had to make his death real, his life real, to take his photo off the piano, so to speak, and make him into a real person.

So I set off from little Dunedin for Hamburg, and with Hartmut met the others in the group at the airport. Not all were veterans; some, like me, had fathers who had fallen in Russia and wanted to pay their respects, if possible to dedicate the crosses on their fathers' graves. We met with the traditional German formality; we shook hands, and introduced ourselves to one another, but there was no discussion, no real meeting of spirits.

Afterword: A Personal Pilgrimage

As I flew to Saint Petersburg, I was full of curiosity, but also rather apprehensive about what might await me. I was conscious that we would be crossing in the comfort of plane and buses the territory my father had traversed on exhausting marches, often right through the night. At Saint Petersburg we saw the Piskarevskoye Memorial Cemetery where one and a half million Russian civilians and soldiers were buried, victims of illness and starvation, as well as of the fighting. I could not get a handle on the incredible number of the dead, nor begin to imagine the suffering of the survivors. It was all too much. Then we headed for Novgorod, visiting several cemeteries on the way; I had no sadness in me, more a sort of awkward shyness, I was not yet able to connect emotionally with the events of this war-torn country.

We reached Ilmensee, Lake Il'men. My mother had often named the place. I knew we were now very close to where my father had fought and died. I sensed his closeness, and secretly wished that he could have found a resting place in the German cemetery on the shores of the lake. This lake had accompanied me throughout my life; I had felt it pulling me towards it. Perhaps a visit to its shores would let me come to terms with the untimely death of the father whom I had missed from childhood, right on into adulthood. It was a peaceful scene—hard to imagine that fifty years ago Russian and German soldiers had been preparing for battle here. I couldn't help wondering what our fellow travelers, the thirty-seven war veterans, must be feeling now, and wishing that my father had survived to be among them. With all my heart I prayed that this idyllic place might never experience war again! For three and a half years the Front had run through this area. One million Russian and German soldiers had died around here. Many had never been properly buried. Now volunteers from all over the world were helping to search for the remains. I tried to digest the fact that in the course of Operation Barbarossa 20 million Russians had died, 2.2 million German soldiers. Unthinkable.

We arrived at Staraja Russa. What did I know about this town of forty thousand inhabitants? Very little. It was, though, the gateway to our personal quest, our search for our father. A Russian driver, Alexander, volunteered to take us to the village of Borki where Vati (Dad) had died. We traveled through impenetrable birch forests with their elks, bears, and wild pigs; it was summer: time for raspberries, blueberries, mossberries, and mushrooms. The land was flat; forest, bog, and moor. We stopped at Parfina, a Russian soldiers' cemetery, and I was deeply moved by the sight of rusty old helmets on top of humps of piled up earth, mass graves, and here and there a wreath. The sordid reality of war was obvious: everything raw, no attempt to beautify the graves.

We came across the deserted village of Tuganova, a landscape of sadness, desolation, and melancholy, despite the sunshine. So much death.

I thought of traditional Māori blessings, of John Donne's "Death be not proud . . .," of Saint John Chrysostom AD 390:

> He whom we love
> And lose
> Is no longer where he was before.
> He is now
> Wherever we are.

Our guide, Raissa, persuaded the bus driver to maneuver the big bus along the rough roads to Borki. It was 3:45 p.m. when we arrived. We parked on a big open space with a few wooden houses around it. Where was the church, I wondered, whose tower my father was supposed to have climbed to check if the village was clear of partisans or enemy forces? Letters testified that he had been killed on leaving the church. We met an old deaf man and his wife, and tried to explain who we were, using words like njemets *(Germans) and* utaroja mrovaia voyna *(Second World War). A glimmer of understanding appeared on his face, and he told us, yes, there had been two churches here. He returned to his garden, to dig his potatoes.*

While people stood around, not knowing what to do next, I took the opportunity to walk around on my own and find a big, supportive tree, a birch, which hid me from the group, and let the floods of overwhelming feelings of sadness, disappointment, and grief have their way with me. I am at my father's death place. This is hallowed ground. In this brief moment of solitude, letting the sandy soil slip between my fingers, I greet my father, meet him, and at the same time bid him farewell.

Somehow it is not so important anymore to find an actual grave. In my grief I find a connectedness with my father and can accept his death. Boarding the bus again I feel a comforting hand on my shoulder, another fellow pilgrim; he has not found the grave of his brother, either.

The next morning Alexander drives me in his twenty-eight-year-old Lada to the nearest Russian Orthodox church. Was this the church on whose tower my father stood with Lieutenant Kreft to be given the Iron Cross? A frail old woman stands at the entrance. I hand her some kopeks and she blesses me. Inside we join the standing worshippers, all women with headscarves. I can light a candle for my father and join in the Divine Liturgy. The smell of

Afterword: A Personal Pilgrimage

poverty hangs in the air, so familiar to me from the Edinburgh slums where I had taught. The choir sings; my thoughts are with my father.

Back in Borki we walk through the village by the river Pola. Our presence has been noticed by the occupants of a house, hidden by three old trees. Alexander points to the oak, the willow, and the elm: "Your father would have seen these trees too," he says. Remarkable, such empathy. A retired teacher, Galina, is standing in the afternoon sun on the village square, now a wasteland; she explains that this place once held two churches, one wooden, and the other stone. The German army burnt one building down; the other was destroyed by the Bolsheviks. After the fierce fighting the villagers had hastily buried the dead.

Galina tells us how before the fighting began, the peasants had shown the soldiers how to build log cabins without a single nail, while the Germans made toys for the children, and ran puppet shows; a German doctor operated on the hands of a thirteen-year-old girl who had picked up a mine from the road. The enemy had shown a human face. We leave with friendly smiles. I am introduced to Ludmilla, who had come to the village in the 1960s, long after the war. She fills all available pockets with early apples from her garden. Borki has become real; the former enemy territory has become a place of friendship, of forgiveness, and mutual reconciliation. I harbor the secret hope and longing that my visit to Borki and my memories of this sleepy, impoverished village, with its shrinking population, may connect my children and grandchildren with their grandfather and great-grandfather. How good if I could be the connection person across generations, could span the distance from Russia to Scotland to New Zealand!

Poems by Laurence Binyon, by John Donne occur to me:

> Surely the Lord is in this place . . .
> No foes nor friends
> But one equal communion.

We return to Saint Petersburg, fly on to Hamburg. I place the Borki apples and the Borki soil on a plate on the table. I try to put the Borki experience into words, to make Ludmilla and Galina and Alexander come alive, and try to evoke the mood of this summer day in Borki, the warmth of the sandy earth, the calmness of the day, and the thoughtfulness of these three Russian people, who allowed me to be sad, who gave me time to grieve for this German *pagip* (soldier)—who died here in the winter of 1942, just thirty years old.

LOVE AND TERROR IN THE THIRD REICH

In Hamburg Hartmut, my cousin Ernst-Otto, his wife, Elke, and I read letters written by my father to his family, letters found in his sister Leni's desk after her death. Leni was Ernst-Otto's mother. Elke notices that I am calmer now than when I left for Borki. I have said my goodbyes; I am at peace.

Yet: once beauty's arrow has hit home, / the pain of love will never end.

(Ewig währt der Schmerz der Liebe). August von Platen.

On my return to my Bonn, I arrived at the Seniorenheim *(my mother's rest home)* by the Rhine, carrying my apples; Mutti lay in her bed. "Ich hab was mitgebracht *(I've brought something with me),*" I said. *The smell of the apples fills the room. Borki is here. The reality of the whole undertaking came home.* "There is nothing there," she had said when we set off for Borki. *But the apples and the soil from Borki spoke another language. It had been no fantasy, but a* sinnvolle Sache *(a sensible undertaking), deeply meaningful for her daughter.*

Indeed for me the return to Bonn and to my home in New Zealand was the beginning, not the end of my engagement with Borki, with my father. In an effort to understand my father, my mother, the war, the pain, and the whole tragedy I began to read countless books about the Third Reich, about the experiences of the men and women like my parents, of die vergessene Generation *(the forgotten generation),* the children of the fallen fathers and the bereaved mothers, the Kriegskinder (war children). I devoured whatever was published about it. I knew now of the letters in the cupboard next to my mother's bed in the old folks' home. But I had no chance to read them until at her death I came across them, and was utterly overwhelmed and astonished by their number and inaccessibility, in this alien Sütterlin script.

My brother, Hartmut, had amassed countless books about National Socialism and about the war. But his interest was in the military campaigns, the politics, and the racist and delusionist policies of National Socialism; he was not able to talk about the letters, the human face of the tragedy. He didn't see the letters as Urkunden *(documentation of the past).* He wasn't interested in keeping them. "Nimm sie mit *(Take them),*" he said, when I indicated my fascination. Fortunately the pastor who conducted my mother's funeral supported me. "These are precious documents." His parents' letters were precious to him. As I began to transcribe the letters, Hartmut, too, was able to help me with some of my questions, as, to a much greater extent, were my cousin, Ernst-Otto and his wife, Elke. But that is another story.

Appendix

Family Tree

Paul Struck m. Herta Krüger   August Sommer m. Frieda Runge
↓   ↓
Lilo (b. 1913), Dieter   Ernst (b. 1912), Leni, Tudi, Hans

Lilo Struck m. Ernst Sommer (1938)
↓
Heinke (b. 1939) & Hartmut (b. 1940)

Bibliography

Archival Sources

Letters by Ernst and Lilo Sommer. 1935–42. Transcribed by Heinke Sommer-Matheson. Hocken Library, Dunedin, New Zealand.

Songbooks, Poetry Anthologies, and Children's Books

Bars, Richard. *Michel Hannemanns Traum*. Charlottenburg: Vaterländischer Frauen-Verein, 1916.
Bohatta-Morpurga, Ida. *Heinzel Wandert durch das Jahr*. Munich: Müller, 1943.
Busch, Wilhelm. *Max und Moritz: Eine Bubengeschichte*. Munich: Braun & Schneider, 1935.
Busch-Schumann, Ruthild, ed. *Guten Abend, Gut' Nacht! Die Schönsten Wiegenlieder*. Mainz: Scholz, 1939.
Heinrich, Richard (illustrator), and Albert Sextus (versifier). *Der Zuckertütenbaum ein Bilderbuch*. Leipzig: Hegel & Schade, 1928.
Fritz Jöde, ed. *Der Musikant: Lieder für die Schule*. Berlin: Kallmeyer, 1930.
Füge, Ernst. *Das Hullebulletöpflein*. Reichenau: Schneider, 1937.
Georg, H. W., ed. *Andersens Schönste Märchen*. Berlin: Weichert, 1898.
Henssel, Walther, ed. *Das Aufrecht Fähnlein: Liederbuch für Studenten und Volk*. Kassel: Bärenreiter, 1934.
Hirt, Ferdinand, ed. *Tausend Sterne Leuchten: Hirts Sammlung Deutscher Gedichte: 2–4 Schuljahr*. Illustrated by Else Wenz-Viëtor. 2nd ed. Breslau: Hirt, 1935.
———, ed. *Tausendstimmiges Leben: Hirts Sammlung Deutscher Gedichte*. 3rd ed. Breslau: Hirt, 1932.
Hoffmann, Heinrich. *Der Struwwelpeter*. 396 ed. Frankfurt: Rütten & Loening, 1917.
Hoffmann, Joseph, ed. *Singendes Volk: Schleswig-Holstein*. Frankfurt: Diesterweg, 1929–1930.
Hollriede, Hagdis. *Weiß dir und mir ein Schönes Haus*. Reichenau: Schneider, 1941.
Jäkel, Erwin. *Für dich und mich!* Dresden: Thienemann, 1930.
Junghändel, Curt. *Soldatenspiel*. N.p., 1940.

BIBLIOGRAPHY

Kempin, Lely. *Die Heilige Insel: Eine Sommergeschichte*. Abbildungen nach Lichtbildern der Verfassserin 20. 14th ed. Bielefeld: Velhagen & Klasing, 1925.
Köhler, Martin, and Karl Wagner. *Perlguckelchen und Weißmäuschen*. Berlin: Verlag der Schriftenvertriebsanstalt, 1898.
Künneth, Walther, *Antwort auf den Mythus. Die Entscheidung zwischen dem nordischen Mythus und dem biblischen Christus*. Berlin: Wichern, 1935.
Mee, Arthur, ed. *The Children's Encyclopaedia*. 8 vols. London: Educational Book Company, 1910.
Neuendorff, Edmund, ed. *Volker Liederbuch*. Leipzig: Eberhardt, 1930.
Niethammer, Vera. *Bei Gacks und Andere Geschichten für Kleine Leute*. Stuttgart: Evangelische Gesellschaft, 1916.
Pallmann, Gerhard, ed. *Wohlauf Kameraden!* Kassel: Bärenreiter, 1934
Presber, Rudolf. *Vater ist im Kriege*. Berlin: Hillger, 1915.
Probst, Hans. *Die Weihnachtsengelein*. Mainz: Thienemann, 1940.
Reichsjugendführung, ed. *Unser Liederbuch: Lieder der Hitler-Jugend*. Munich: NSDAP Zentralverlag, 1939.
Reichsverwaltung des NS.-Lehrerbundes. *Küken Steigt ins Leben*. Hilf-mit!-Schriftenreihe 10. Berlin-Tempelhof: Braun, 1938.
Schirach, Baldur Benedikt von, ed. *Blut und Ehre: Lieder der Hitler-Jugend*. Berlin: Deutscher Jugendverlag, 1933.
Simrock, Karl, ed. *Reineke Fuchs (Reynard the Fox)*. Bunte Jugendbücher 37. Reutlingen: Ensslin & Laiblin, 1923.
Storm, Theodor. *Der kleine Häwelmann*. Oldenburg: Stalling, 1926.

Secondary Sources

Arendt, Hannah. *The Origins of Totalitarianism*. San Diego: Harcourt, Brace & World, 1968.
Bauer, Josef. *290. Infanterie Division: Weg und Schicksal*. Delmenhorst: Kameraden-Hilfswerk, 1960.
Bentley, James. *Martin Niemöller*. New York: Free Press, 1985.
Bergen, Doris L. *The Twisted Cross: The German Christian Movement in the Third Reich*. Chapel Hill: University of North Carolina Press, 1996.
Bessel, Richard, ed., with an introduction. *Life in the Third Reich*. Oxford: Oxford University Press, 2001.
Boberach, Heinz. *Meldungen aus dem Reich*. DTV-Taschenbücher 477. Munich: DTV, 1968.
Brecht, Bertolt. *The Fear and Misery of the Third Reich*. Translated by John Willett. Methuen Modern Plays. London: Methuen Drama, 2002.
Davidson, Martin. *The Perfect Nazi: Unmasking My SS Grandfather*. London: Viking, 2010.
Ericksen, Robert P. *Theologians under Hitler: Gerhard Kittel, Paul Althaus, and Emanuel Hirsch*. New Haven: Yale University Press, 1985.
Evans, Richard. *The Third Reich at War*. London: Lane, 2008.
———. *The Third Reich in Power*. London: Lane, 2005.
Friedländer, Saul. *The Years of Extermination*. Nazi Germany and the Jews, 1939–1945 2. 2 vols. London: Weidenfeld & Nicholson, 2008.

Bibliography

Gutteridge, Richard. *Open Thy Mouth for the Dumb! The German Evangelical Church and the Jews, 1879-1950*. Oxford: Blackwell, 1976.

Hahn, Ulla. *Unscharfe Bilder: Roman*. Munich: Deutsche Verlags-Anstalt, 2003.

Heidenreich, Gisela. *Das Endlose Jahr: Die Langsame Entdeckung der Eigenen Biographie*. Frankfurt: Fischer, 2004.

Helmreich, Ernst Christian. *The German Churches under Hitler: Background, Struggle, and Epilogue* Detroit: Wayne State University Press, 1979.

Hölderlin, Friedrich. "Celebration of Peace" (*Friedensfeier*). In *Sämtliche Werke*, 2:425–32. 6 Bände. Stuttgart; Kohlhammer, 1953.

Hürter, Johannes. *Ein Deutscher General an der Ostfront: Die Briefe und Tagebücher des Gotthard Heinrici 1941–42*. Edition Tempus. Erfurt: Sutton, 2001.

Katzenelson, Itzhak. *Großer Gesang vom Ausgerotteten Jüdischen Volk*. Translated by Wolf Biermann. Cologne: Kiepenheuer & Witsch, 1994.

Kempowski, Walter. *Das Echolot-Ein Kollektives Tagebuch: Januar und Februar 1943*. 2nd ed. Munich: Knaus, 1993.

———. *Das Echolot. Barbarossa '41. Ein Kollektives Tagebuch*. 5th ed. Munich: Random House, 2004.

Lepenies, Wolf. *The Seduction of Culture in German History*. Princeton: Princeton University Press, 2006.

Leppien, Annemarie, and Jörn-Peter Leppien. *Mädel-Landjahr in Schleswig-Holstein: Einblicke in ein Kapitel Nationalsozialistischer Mädchenerziehung 1936-1940*. Neumünster: Wachholtz, 1989.

Littell, Jonathan. *The Kindly Ones*. London: Vintage, 2010.

MacGregor, Neil. *Germany: Memories of a Nation*. London: Lane, 2014.

Mann, Golo. *Deutsche Geschichte 1919-1945*. Fischer Bücherei 387. Frankfurt: Fischer, 1962.

Matheson, Peter. "Christian Churches and the Jews in the Third Reich: Words and Silences." *Interface Theology* 1 (2015) 1–18.

———. "The Christian Churches and the Jews in the Third Reich." *Judaica* 27 (1971) 132–46.

———. "Luther and Hitler: A Controversy Reviewed." *Journal of Ecumenical Studies* 17 (1980) 445–53.

———, ed. *The Third Reich and the Christian Churches*. Edinburgh: T. & T. Clark, 1981.

Milne, Esther. *Letters, Postcards, Email: Technologies of Presence*. Routledge Research in Cultural and Media studies 24. New York: Routledge, 2010.

Noakes, Jeremy, ed. *The German Home Front in World War II*. Documents in Nazism 1919-1945 4. Exeter Studies in History 6. Exeter: University of Exeter Press, 1998.

Robinson, Gabrielle. *The Reluctant Nazi*. Stroud: History Press, 2012.

Rollin, Marion. "'Gott schuf keine Stände, keine Klassen, aber Rassen': Einblicke in die Kirchengemeinde Blankenese während der Zeit des Nationalsozialismus." Lecture delivered at the Historical Association for Research into Jews in Blankenese, Hamburg, Germany, on May 12, 2004.

Roseman, Mark. *The Past in Hiding*. London: Lane, 2000.

Rosenberg, Alfred. *Der Mythus des 20. Jahrhunderts*. 32 ed. Munich: Hoheneichen, 1930.

Scholder, Klaus. *The Churches and the Third Reich*. 2 vols. Eugene OR: Wipf & Stock, 2018.

Stargardt, Nicholas. *The German War: A Nation under Arms, 1939-45*. London: Bodley Head, 2015.

Bibliography

Timms, Edward. *Anna Haag and Her Secret Diary of the Second World War: A Democratic German Feminist's Response to the Catastrophe of National Socialism*. Women in German literature 20. Oxford: Lang, 2016.

Vinen, Richard. *The Unfree French: Life under the Occupation*. New Haven: Yale University Press, 2006.

www.ingramcontent.com/pod-product-compliance
Lightning Source LLC
Chambersburg PA
CBHW022114160426
43197CB00009B/1023